CRYSTAL THERAPY

Also by Doreen Virtue, Ph.D.

Books/Kit/Oracle Board

ANGEL GUIDANCE ORACLE BOARD
GODDESSES & ANGELS
CONNECTING WITH YOUR ANGELS KIT (includes booklet, CD, journal, etc.)
ANGEL MEDICINE
THE CRYSTAL CHILDREN
ARCHANGELS & ASCENDED MASTERS
EARTH ANGELS
MESSAGES FROM YOUR ANGELS
ANGEL VISIONS II
EATING IN THE LIGHT (with Becky Prelitz, M.F.T., R.D.)
THE CARE AND FEEDING OF INDIGO CHILDREN
HEALING WITH THE FAIRIES
ANGEL VISIONS
DIVINE PRESCRIPTIONS
HEALING WITH THE ANGELS
"I'D CHANGE MY LIFE IF I HAD MORE TIME"
DIVINE GUIDANCE
CHAKRA CLEARING (available in tradepaper, and as a hardcover book-with-CD)
ANGEL THERAPY
THE LIGHTWORKER'S WAY
CONSTANT CRAVING A–Z
CONSTANT CRAVING
THE YO-YO DIET SYNDROME
LOSING YOUR POUNDS OF PAIN

Oracle Cards

HEALING WITH THE ANGELS ORACLE CARDS
HEALING WITH THE FAIRIES ORACLE CARDS
MESSAGES FROM YOUR ANGELS ORACLE CARDS (card deck and booklet)
MAGICAL MERMAIDS AND DOLPHINS ORACLE CARDS (card deck and booklet)
ARCHANGEL ORACLE CARDS (card deck and booklet)
GODDESS GUIDANCE ORACLE CARDS (card deck and booklet)
MAGICAL UNICORNS ORACLE CARDS (card deck and booklet)
SAINTS & ANGELS (card deck and booklet)

❀

All of the above are available at your local bookstore,
or may be ordered by visiting: Hay House USA: **www.hayhouse.com®;**
Hay House Australia: **www.hayhouse.com.au;** Hay House UK:
www.hayhouse.co.uk • Hay House South Africa:
www.hayhouse.co.za; Hay House India: **www.hayhouse.co.in**

Doreen's Website: **www.AngelTherapy.com**
Judith's Website: **www.CrystalFriends.com**

CRYSTAL THERAPY

How to Heal and Empower Your Life
with Crystal Energy

Doreen Virtue, Ph.D.,
and Judith Lukomski

HAY HOUSE, INC.

Carlsbad, California • New York City
London • Sydney • Johannesburg
Vancouver • Hong Kong • New Delhi

Published and distributed in the United States by: Hay House, Inc.: www.hayhouse.com
• *Published and distributed in Australia by:* Hay House Australia Pty. Ltd.:
www.hayhouse.com.au • *Published and distributed in the United Kingdom by:* Hay
House UK, Ltd.: www.hayhouse.co.uk • *Published and distributed in the Republic
of South Africa by:* Hay House SA (Pty), Ltd.: www.hayhouse.co.za • *Distributed
in Canada by:* Raincoast: www.raincoast.com • *Published in India by:* Hay House
Publishers India: www.hayhouse.co.in

Editorial supervision: Jill Kramer   *Design:* Amy Rose Grigoriou
Interior photos: **www.photographybycheryl.com**

Library of Congress Cataloging-in-Publication Data

Virtue, Doreen.
  Crystal therapy : how to heal and empower your life with crystal energy /
Doreen Virtue and Judith Lukomski.
     p. cm.
  Includes bibliographical references.
  ISBN 1-4019-0467-X (tradepaper)
  1. Crystals—Psychic aspects. I. Lukomski, Judith, 1960- II. Title.
  BF1442.C78V57 2005
  133'.2548—dc22
                              2004008603

ISBN 13: 978-1-4019-0467-8
ISBN 10: 1-4019-0467-X

14 13 12 11   12 11 10 9
1st printing, January 2005
9th printing, January 2011

Printed in China

Contents

An
Introduction
to Crystal
Therapy

Crystals are powerful healing tools, and you can use them to boost your natural spiritual healing power. In this book, you'll learn how to select stones (we use the words *stones* and *crystals* interchangeably) to help you heal every area of your life. Crystals can help with your physical, emotional, spiritual, and financial health; and they can support your romantic life, help you and your children sleep better, amplify your healing power, and assist you in feeling happy and peaceful.

Crystals are the offspring of Heaven and Earth's marriage. They're a gift from Gaia, the spirit of our planet, to amplify the power of light and love. No matter what type of healing work you're involved in, crystals can help. Our prayer is that, through this book, you'll discover the loving energy emanating from crystals.

Although they may seem like inert objects, crystals are very much alive. They're both *filled* with energy, and are *conduits* of energy. That's one reason why crystals are used in watches, radios, and modern medical devices.

In this book, you'll read channeled messages from the crystals in order to familiarize you with the voice of the crystal kingdom. You'll find that this work functions as a guidebook for both beginners and seasoned veterans of crystal healing. If you'd like to know which crystal to use for a particular life issue, you'll find charts that list the specialties of the more commonly available stones, and you'll read simple definitions of the terms associated with crystals (such as *double-terminated,* for instance). You'll also find out how the geometric shape and cut of your crystal affects its energy, and discover fascinating information about *how* crystals are mined—and why that process affects your personal stone and its energy.

Crystal Therapy

Crystals amplify their *own* energy, as well as the Divine universal energy that has different names, including *Spirit,*

Introduction

chi, qi, prana, Light and Love, and *Reiki.* The term *crystal therapy* refers to working with crystals' live energy and voice in conjunction with Divine energy. Crystal therapy helps you to better hear, feel, and know the voice of Spirit during your healing sessions. The crystals work especially by assisting you in healing and helping you communicate with your guardian angels. Since crystal therapy is an intuitive healing process, it's normal for psychic ability to increase as you work with the stones.

Our experience with this type of therapy has taught us that crystals are alive and filled with exciting and healing messages for us all. They have so much to share with us if we'll only listen. For that reason, we refer to crystals as *crystal friends* throughout this book, and speak of them as beings instead of objects. Part of our mission is to increase awareness of the gifts that our friends from the crystal kingdom have for us all. All we ask is that you keep an open mind about this subject. After all, everything in the Universe is composed of ever-moving atomic particles, and God is everywhere. Therefore, God is within crystals, and the atoms of all crystals are quite active.

You can probably feel major shifts surging through the world today. As the world speeds up, it's natural for you to want to slow down and ground yourself. Well, crystals can help you do both. They can help you understand all the new world energies by opening spiritual channels for you, while also reconnecting you to Mother Earth.

These remarkable beings of the rock clan are present on Earth to assist us in remembering the dynamics of evolution. As we acknowledge and accept these wise friends, we begin experiencing their positive influence. They've been patiently awaiting our willingness to interact from a place of integrity and truth, to assist us in healing old patterns while escalating our sensitivity to timeless knowledge.

When did *you* first notice a stone, feel the inclination to pick it up, and discover a vibration pulsating through your hand? Judith recalls, "My initiation came as a young child of less than five years old, sitting outside in the summer warmth near the family pool. I was mesmerized by glints of sunshine captured in the rocks. They sparkled in the light, winking at me in recognition. Fascinated, I learned that each was a friend that provided guidance, healing, and comfort. It was the beginning of a spectacular lifelong relationship with the mineral kingdom."

With crystal therapy, Heaven and nature have come together to create a vast array of combinations and structures. As you read this book, remember that the mineral kingdom happily welcomes you to explore the beauty, power, and joy of crystals.

CHAPTER ONE

A KINSHIP WITH CRYSTALS

Crystals aren't "New Age"—they've always been a part of our 4.6-billion-year-old planet. And you've most likely worked with them in other lifetimes. So, they feel familiar to you and you instinctively know how to work with them. The Crystal Children (the new sensitive and psychic babies and toddlers) are showing a remarkable knowledge of healing with crystals—without being taught. This inherent wisdom comes partly from the many lifetimes that crystals have served as jewelry, healing tools, and friends to all inhabitants of the planet.

Have you ever considered how your life is touched by the renaissance of crystals in today's culture? Modern technology uses ancient natural crystals to boost radio waves and for "newly" discovered vibrational medicine using crystal energy. Home décor stores sell crystals as decorations, and powdered crystals are ingredients in mainstream beauty products (as they were in ancient Egypt). Mineral awareness is soaring, and acceptance of crystal power is growing, so it's the perfect time to practice crystal therapy.

Crystals are usually associated with ancient wisdom and heavenly caverns of mystery and magic. That's because crystals are record-keepers and storehouses of memories and knowledge about the earth's spiritual healing history. Crystals bring up familiar memories of enormous dazzling quartz points and crystal healing beds used in ancient Atlantis, Lemuria, and other civilizations. Our shared recollections of ancient times now urge us to reconnect with the angelic and mineral kingdoms, to unlock ageless knowledge, and remember healing aspects of nature that support humankind's ongoing evolution.

Crystals are members of the mineral kingdom in the physical world. In the spiritual world, they belong to the "elemental realm," which encompasses the spirits that guard, heal, and protect the planet. Other members of the elemental realm include fairies, dolphins, elves, and leprechauns. You can see the faces of the "stone and mineral people" as you look at boulders and squares of marble tiles.

These beings are "nature angels," who are denser than guardian angels. Density means that the beings' energy vibrates at a slower rate, enabling us to see and feel them with our physical senses. Elementals, plants, animals, and humans are the densest energetically because they inhabit the heavy physical energy of the earth. This density makes it easier to feel, see, and hear nature angels (fairies, tree spirits, crystals, and such) than celestial angels. And since our bodies and our diet are composed of minerals, we're communing with our cousins when we work with the crystals.

We're entering a new phase in our relationship with Earth, with increased awareness and respect for the delicate balance between the environment and humankind. Crystals are vocal spokespersons for the planet, reminiscent of the tiny "Whos" in the legendary Dr. Seuss book, *Horton Hears a Who!* In the book, an elephant named Horton was about to unknowingly ingest a civilization of "Whos." All the Whos decided to scream loudly so that Horton would be aware of them and not eat them and their "planet." Yet, Horton couldn't hear the Whos until one tiny young Who added his voice.

Perhaps your own personal crystal will be the voice that helps all of humanity hear the pleas of Mother Earth, who wants to be treated kindly and with respect.

Our Old Friends, the Crystals

The haunting beauty of the mineral kingdom is irresistible, so it's no wonder that the human race has a long history of wearing and working with crystals. Historians and archaeologists have traced the use of crystals in healing and beauty rituals back to the earliest civilizations. And no wonder: They magnify personal and planetary vibrational energy. Our ancestors used crystals as mystical tools, energy generators, communication enhancers, and medical instruments. Archaeological digs show their use as talismans of good fortune and protection; as well as amulets, jewelry, and magnificent home showpieces.

Each society has contributed unique stories to the world related to their use of stones. From India to the Americas, we find examples of the interest in, and application of, crystals throughout literature, science, culture, and myth. For instance, legend says that a gem city once existed in the Greek Isles, with walls of emerald, streets paved with gold, and temples housing huge amethyst altars used for prayer and the like. The Bible, in the book of Exodus, speaks of jewels in the High Priests' breastplates, which assisted their relationship with the Divine. In the Far East, exquisitely crafted precious stones encrusted in gold spoke of wealth and status for those who wore them as jewelry.

Gems and zodiac correlations surface in documentation of the Native American Medicine Wheel, as well as in the Ayurvedic and Western astrological systems, and continue to be referenced and integrated by modern-day cultures. Native Americans knew of the powerful healing attributes of stones and metals, such as turquoise and silver, which aided in the healing of physical, emotional, and etheric bodies.

Modern indigenous cultures still use crystals in their spiritual practices. For example, Australian Aborigines perform rituals that include stone and sound vibration using the didgeridoo (a large bamboo trumpet) and rocks painted with sacred designs in order to help them connect with Source through dreamtime journeys. Shamans of Europe and the Pacific Islands often invoked the power of stones to ease suffering and provide release in healing ceremonies.

The most famous crystal association may be Atlantis, where crystal vibrations helped create a society blessed with astonishing technological advances exceeding those of our modern day. There are many legends of Atlantean flying machines, healing beds, and perpetual lighting instruments that were solely fueled by crystals. Mystics such as Edgar Cayce, Ruth Montgomery, and Dolores Cannon have discussed the double-edged sword of crystal power in Atlantis. Some Atlantean leaders decided to use crystals as powerful weapons to forcefully conquer other countries. Legend says that this misuse of crystal power eventually exploded the heart of the Atlantean civilization.

This topic dovetails with two of Plato's dialogues: *Timaeus* and *Critias,* both written in 360 B.C. Plato received his information about Atlantis from Critias the Younger, the grandson of a Greek ruler named Solon, who learned about Atlantis while visiting Egypt in 590 B.C. In these dialogues, Plato discusses the sudden demise of Atlantis. Whether the explosion came from misused crystals or from a volcano (as some modern theorists believe), we're now recalling the connection that Atlantis had with crystals' remarkable healing power. Doreen wrote about the Atlantean crystals healing beds and temples in her book *Angel Medicine* (Hay House, 2004).

We believe that the interest in crystals is resurging as part of the spiritual renaissance and the ascension process we're all undergoing. As you read about Atlantean crystals, do you feel a familiarity deep within your being? If so, your purpose may involve preventing this world from repeating the mistakes made by Atlanteans as they sought domination of the world's resources. This is a critical time in our history, and it's imperative that we create harmonious change.

We're obviously not the first individuals to unveil the capabilities found in the mineral kingdom. However, let's be the first to consciously embrace their abilities with a purity of intent. Asking for Heaven's help, by connecting with the angelic realm while working in focused partnership with the mineral family, ensures a potent interaction based in love and grace. This combination of realms, celestial and elemental, blends the power of Heaven and Earth to create a magical formula of healing. Let us now choose to embrace the best of both worlds.

CHAPTER TWO

CRYSTALS AND SACRED GEOMETRY

Crystalline structures reflect the perfection of the Universe in earthly manifestation. The Greeks were one of the first cultures to realize this vital link. The word *crystal* comes from the Greek words *krystallos* and *kryos,* meaning "ice" and " icy cold." This ancient interpretation is close to the truth, since quartz is cool to the touch and looks like sparkling ice captured in stone.

The Greek philosopher Pythagoras uncovered basic mathematical symmetries found in music and physical form. In his quest to comprehend the Universe, he discovered three key shapes in matter: the tetrahedron, the hexahedron, and the dodecahedron. He found these natural congruities as a pattern within math, language, music, and science. His discovery showed that matter is built upon perfect forms comprised of equilateral, equiangular polygons (closed plane figures bounded by straight lines, with equal sides and angles).

One hundred and fifty years later, Plato's student Theaetetus determined two additional shapes (the octahedron and icosahedron) as part of the basic structures of form. His conclusion was reached from continued research of the original Pythagorean theorem. The combination of these shapes creates what are known as the *Platonic Solids.*

Plato later linked the designated shapes with the earth's four elements: fire, water, earth, and air. The fifth shape represents spirit, or the nonmaterial and metaphysical. Here are the five shapes of the Platonic Solids:

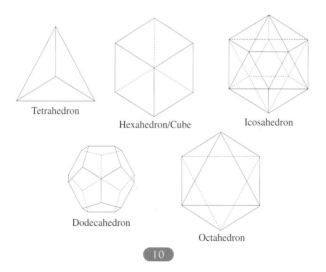

Tetrahedron

Hexahedron/Cube

Icosahedron

Dodecahedron

Octahedron

Shape	No. of Faces	No. of Vertices	No. of Edges	Element
Tetrahedron	4	4	6	Fire
Hexahedron/ Cube	6	8	12	Earth
Octahedron	8	6	12	Air
Dodecahedron	12	20	30	Spirit
Icosahedron	20	12	30	Water

The Platonic Solids serve as a key to sacred geometry and the numeric formula of Divine design. Ancient Greeks would meditate upon these five shapes in order to access spiritual wisdom and guidance. Today, we can still see the tetrahedron shapes of the world's pyramids, which were also used as focal points for gathering and building spiritual energy.

These symmetrical forms are repeated in every part of life—from snowflakes to DNA strands, from architecture to soccer balls. Crystals embody these shapes: They're spirit, energy, and sacred geometry in material form—birthed from Mother Earth.

The Origins and Growth of Crystals

In any relationship, getting to know one another is full of exciting discoveries and shared experiences that enhance your long-term rapport. Learning about crystal families can create a similar appreciation, strengthening the union between you (as the guardian) and your precious stone. As you gain awareness with respect to the formation and composition of crystals, you also acquire insight into planetary DNA and the dynamics of creation, deepening both personal and global crystalline connection.

Heaven and Earth have come together, graciously producing these crystal beings through cosmic delivery—such as tektite stones (the family name for meteorites), which create a great connection with the extraterrestrial realms—and through the earth's geological structure.

The earth is comprised of three basic layers: core, mantle, and crust. The most extreme heat is found at the center of the earth or core, followed by the mantle, where internal temperatures are less concentrated than in the coolest area, which is referred to as the crust. It's within these three layers that magma (molten rock) is formed, cooled, and mixed with water to create distinctive deposits of igneous, metamorphic, and sedimentary rocks.

Typically, there are four ways in which these deposits are formed:

1. **Crystallization,** in which elements combine under extreme temperatures to create minerals as they cool.

2. **Recrystallization,** or the second time a mineral is formed under severe temperature and pressure, creating a new chemical reaction and generating a different form.

3. **Precipitation** from aqueous solutions (water), in which elements mix and move, interacting with one another to develop a new chemical configuration. Opal is formed from this process.

4. **Chemical alterations,** in which changing natural conditions cultivate new combinations. For instance, malachite is formed through the oxidation of chalcopyrite (copper).

As you can see, minerals form in a wide range of environments, blending chemical ingredients, pressures, and temperatures to create a specific stone through the mechanisms of plate tectonics (movements of earth sections as the sea floor spreads, which is associated with continental drift).

Crystals, Minerals, Rocks, and Gems

As you work with crystals, you'll hear a lot of terms that can seem confusing and complicated at first. Yet, as you get to know the origins of stones, you'll soon understand the differences between crystals, minerals, rocks, and gemstones.

Some of their basic distinguishing characteristics follow:

- **Crystals** often refer to clear quartz formations, yet they're also the minuscule forms of chemical elements.

- **Minerals** are chemical elements with a separate constitution, such as salt or sulphur.

- **Rocks and stones** are combinations of minerals formed from a unique mix of elements and environmental circumstances.

- **Gemstones** are described as semiprecious or precious based upon their color, availability, and mining requirements. The four most precious stones are the emerald, diamond, ruby, and sapphire.

Although there are more than 100 gemstones and several thousand mineral shapes, they can be categorized using a seven-system format that was created by French scientist René-Just Haüy in the late 18th century, just as *crystallography,* the study of crystals, developed.

The crystallography system comes from the understanding that rocks develop through natural atomic forces that create the symmetrical exterior faces of a crystal. The mineral is put into a specific system based on the number of faces it has.

This may sound complicated, but if you think about it, it makes sense to categorize crystal types. In addition to Haüy's seven groups, most "crystalologists" include two more, which you'll see below. It's not necessary to memorize (or even to completely understand) these categories in order to benefit from crystal therapy and the healing power that crystals bring us.

Crystal Systems	Common Minerals
Cubic	Pyrite, Garnet, Marcasite
Hexagonal	Quartz, Beryl (Aquamarine, Emerald)

Monoclinic	Jade (Jadeite, Nephrite), Selenite
Orthorhombic	Alexandrite, Cat's-Eye
Tetragonal	Zircon, Chalcopyrite (source for copper)
Triclinic	Feldspar, Labradorite, Moonstone
Trigonal	Tourmaline, Quartz, Dioptase
Amorphous/ Noncrystalline	Obsidian, Amber
Organic Forms	Coral, Pearl

Human-made vs. Natural Stones

As you shop for crystals, you may discover that some of them are human-made, while others are created naturally by Mother Earth. In most cases, human-made stones are less expensive, so it can be tempting to buy them for a seemingly bargain price. But before you make that purchase, take a moment to explore their energy. Compare how you feel while holding a human-made stone, after you've held a natural one. You'll probably sense a greater amount of warm, loving energy from the natural stone.

Naturally produced stones are the outpouring of Mother Earth's history, love, and knowledge; and those such as moldavite are gifts from Heaven's cosmic treasure chest. Synthetics can be used in crystal therapy, but it doesn't happen often. Many people find that their energy vibrates differently than it does with the authentic stone. In part, the difference is age: Organically formed stones contain the wisdom of the earth's cycles, while artificial ones have a younger energy. From this perspective, it's important to understand how minerals are formed, mined, and marketed, in conjunction with how they'll be used in your practice of crystal therapy.

Mining vs. Finding

In most mining operations, collecting crystals is an afterthought rather than the primary consideration. The miners are focused on amassing a particular ore or preparing the infrastructure of progress, and if they happen to find crystals along the way, they're gathered.

As the popularity of crystals rises, there's a new trend whereby mines unearth these minerals as their primary objective. In some cases, the miners use explosives to flush them out. No wonder, then, that there's a movement under way to hand-mine stones when possible. Even better is *finding* them, instead of forcibly taking them from the ground. It's no coincidence that environmentalists are adamant about defending the earth, not only on behalf of the animal and plant kingdoms, but also for the mineral family. These wondrous beings need our help—their homes are being destroyed through harsh techniques, including dynamite blasting and chemical infiltration.

You can assist through conscious consumerism, similar to how you shop for organic produce or free-range animal products. Either ask the merchant about the mineral's history, or ask the stone itself: Hold it, close your eyes, and mentally ask it how it was gathered from the earth. Was it through a harsh transaction, or was it lovingly gathered? Trust the answer that you receive.

Fragmented energy can be left in the crystal when a harsh technique has released it from the earth, and you can often feel this residual negativity in its vibration. If you're the guardian of such a stone, cleanse it by setting the intention to access pure energy, and then bless the healing process of both the stone and the earth from which it sprang. In most cases, you'll feel an immediate shift in response.

It's an honor to be a caretaker for crystals. Treat them as you would dear friends; in other words nurture and respect them. Their support strengthens your ability to realize the essence of universal wisdom.

Chapter Three

Putting Crystal Therapy into Form and Practice

Crystals are much more than beautiful ornaments. They're powerful energy conductors, and their gorgeous colors, shapes, and inclusions (foreign substances enclosed in the mineral) all influence how they magnify energies. Since the time of Atlantis, and perhaps before, crystals have been used to conduct healings. Crystals amplify energy in a process called "piezoelectricity," and today, hospitals use quartz crystals, microbalances, and piezoelectric crystal sensors in diagnostic and healing work. Crystals are also routinely found in radios, watches, and other electronic devices. And don't forget that our bodies and diets have high mineral contents, which make these elements part of our earthly family.

If you believe, like we do, that God is omnipresent—everywhere—then the Creator is also within crystals. They have a spirit that's alive, and these "rock people" are loving beings who desire to bring joy, healing, and happiness to you and the planet.

Crystals and Intentions

Crystal therapy is an intuitive way of working with stones to effect healings of all varieties. When you work with the stones, you'll invoke the angels' energy and guidance. You'll also be channeling Divine light through your body, then into the crystal, and into the person or animal receiving the healing energy. This process will likely feel like second nature, as you've probably engaged in a version of crystal therapy in a prior lifetime or during your dreamtime soul travels. You'll rediscover that such therapy is a joyful and uplifting experience for both the healer and the "healee."

As you conduct crystal therapy, keep in mind that your intention sets the tone for the outcome, and because crystals amplify energy, they'll also boost your underlying intention. So, before beginning a healing session, take the time to center and quiet your mind and body. Ask yourself, "What are my intentions with this session?"

Be honest with yourself. For instance, if you sense any motivation to impress others with your "special healing gifts," realize that this is an ego-related intention. There's no shame in it, since everyone falls into such traps occasionally. However, if you work with crystals with the intention of impressing others, then the energy of the underlying fear ("What if they don't like me?") is what will be boosted.

If you find yourself in this situation, focus on the thought, *Archangels Jophiel, Michael, and Raphael, please help me hold pure intentions of light, love, and service.* These angels (described in more detail later on) will help you channel from your Higher Self instead of your ego.

Another ego-based intention that can block healing is the belief that your client is the source of your income. In truth, the light and the love flowing through you and into your client are the Source of all that you need. Approaching a session with a fear of financial lack will put the intentions upon that fear, and diminish the flow of healing energy. There's nothing wrong with accepting money for healing work—in fact, when a client gives you money or some other type of payment, it's a healthy and advisable energy exchange for both parties. However, it's important to understand that compensation is a natural part of the universal law of giving and receiving. It doesn't come *from* your client, it flows *through* him or her from the Source of all.

Also, make sure that you're not handing Heaven a script that says, "I want the healing session to look this way, with these specific results." Outlining your desired results to Heaven can block you from receiving a better or more ingenious outcome, so don't worry about or try to tell the Universe how the healing should occur. Remember that the Divine and infinite wisdom of the Universe often wants more for us than we do for ourselves, and that the Source is also privy to wonderfully creative ways to manifest a healing. Leave "the how" of any healing or manifestation up to God, and you'll enjoy it more, feel less personal strain, and experience more fruitful outcomes.

The best intentions, those that are most conducive to healing and manifestation, include the following:

- To be a clear channel of Divine love and light

- To be of pure service to the being with whom you're working

- To clearly hear, see, feel, and know the angels' guidance during the session

- To be an instrument of healing, with the highest possible outcome, for everyone's best good

- To bring blessings to the world and all who inhabit it

These goals open you up, like the clearest and most powerful crystal, to be a conduit of magnified healing energy. You can also ask your angels, guides, Creator, and Higher Self to guide and cleanse your thoughts. Crystal clear intentions maximize the energy that flows through you and the stone.

Once you've set your desires for the session, you may wonder if you'll know what to do while working with the crystals. Don't worry—instead, trust and have faith that during each moment, you'll be given clear guidance that you can easily understand. The pure intentions that you set have guaranteed a wonderful healing session and outcome.

Calling on Angels

Next, call on your angels for assistance and guidance. For instance, you may silently say, "Divine love and light of creation and healing angels, I call upon you now. Please assist, guide, and protect me in [state your intention for the healing or manifestation]. I ask that your wisdom, love, and light be sent through me and magnified through the crystals for the purposes of healing and the highest will. Thank you."

In addition to your guardian angels, you can call upon the "Crystal Angels"—angels who specialize in helping us unite with the energy of Divine love within the earth's rock, minerals, and crystals. Judith remembers the first time she connected with a Crystal Angel: "When I first started connecting with crystal energy, I sensed that there was a presence with me. Not just the crystalline frequency, but also energy of celestial lightness surrounding me with love. At first I thought it was my guardian angel or perhaps the archangels, then I came to know 'Crystal' (the name of the particular Crystal Angel who came to me). Her vibration is nurturing, as if Mother Earth has been given form. I see her joyful essence in hues of soft golden light with shades of pink and green, reminding me of rainbow inclusions within a clear quartz crystal when the light dances upon it."

As you practice crystal therapy, invite the Crystal Angels to join you. They'll assist you in making crystal selections and understanding mineral wisdom. Their message is simple yet powerful: *"Relax and breathe. You are surrounded by support from Heaven and Earth. No journey is ever made alone. When you have a question, ask, and you'll receive the knowledge you seek. Trust in your ability to discern what's appropriate for you. Listen with an open heart, for we come to you together with resplendent gems of wisdom, bringing secrets forgotten and now reclaimed."*

The Crystal Angels and your guardian angels will guide you in selecting which crystal to work with during your crystal-therapy session, or you can refer to Chapter 7 or the reference charts in this book to select a stone aligned with your intentions. Your angels will hold your hand, showing you how and where to hold the crystal. This guidance will come in the form of gut feelings, intuition, visions, words, or thoughts. If you have doubts or fears about your abilities, mentally call upon Archangel Michael, who gives us courage and clears away fears. (Just think, *Archangel Michael,* and he'll come to your side immediately—guaranteed.)

You can call upon these angels, the angels of the person to whom you're sending healing energy, the archangels, or a combination. We always believe that the more help that comes to us, the better.

Archangels are the managers of our guardian angels, and they're one type of the nine varieties of angels (which include angels, archangels, principalities, powers, virtues, dominions, thrones, cherubim, and seraphim). Of these nine forms, the angels and archangels are the most involved with helping Earth and her inhabitants.

Archangels are larger and more powerful than angels. They're nonphysical, yet they're very palpable, audible, and visible as you tune in to them. As nonphysical celestial beings, they don't have genders; however, their specific specialties and characteristics give them distinctive male and female energies and personas.

The study and writings about archangels are ancient and nondenominational—in fact, age-old monotheistic spiritual texts list 15 of them. They are sometimes called by different names, but here are the most common ones, along with their specialties and characteristics to help you decide whom to call upon during your crystal-therapy sessions:

- **Ariel** (pronounced "Ar-ee-EL"). Her name means "Lioness of God," and she heals and helps wild animals and the environment

- **Azrael** (pronounced "OZ-ri-el"). His name means "Whom God helps," and he heals grief and helps those who are consoling the bereaved.

- **Chamuel** (pronounced "SHAM-u-el"). His name means "He who sees God." Chamuel heals anxiety, brings global and personal peace; and helps find lost objects, situations, and people.

- **Gabriel** (pronounced "GAB-ree-el"). Her name means "Messenger of God." Gabriel helps and heals during conception; pregnancy and childbirth; heals anxiety regarding creative projects; and especially helps parents, journalists, and orators.

- **Haniel** (pronounced "HAHN-ee-el"). Her name means "Glory of God," and she heals female cycles and helps with clairvoyance.

- **Jeremiel** (pronounced "Jer-EM-i-el"). His name means "Mercy of God." He heals emotions, and helps us review and take inventory of our life so that we may forgive and plan positive changes.

- **Jophiel** (pronounced "JO-fee-el"). Her name means "Beauty of God." Jophiel heals negativity and chaos; and brings beauty and organization to our thoughts, home, office, and other environments.

- **Metatron** (pronounced "Met-ah-TRON"). Formerly the prophet Enoch, Metatron heals learning disorders and childhood issues, and helps with the new Indigo and Crystal Children. (Because they were prophets who ascended to archangeldom, Metatron and Sandalphon don't have literal Hewbrew translations with respect to the meanings of their names.)

- **Michael** (pronounced "MY-kel" or "Mik-ay-EL"). His name means "He who is like God." He releases us from fear and doubt, protects us, and clears away negativity.

- **Raguel** (pronounced "RAG-u-el" or "Rag-UL"). His name means "Friend of God," and he brings harmony to all relationships, and helps heal misunderstandings.

- **Raphael** (pronounced "ROFF-ay-el"). His name means "He who heals." Raphael heals physical illnesses of humans and animals, and guides healers and would-be healers.

- **Raziel** (pronounced "ROZ-ee-el"). His name means "Secrets of God." He heals spiritual and psychic blocks, and helps

us with dream interpretation and past-life
memories.

- **Sandalphon** (pronounced "SAN-dul-fun").
  Formerly the prophet Elijah, Sandalphon
  heals aggressive tendencies, and helps
  musicians and music used for healing
  purposes.

- **Uriel** (pronounced "YUR-ee-el"). His name
  means "God is Light." Uriel heals resent-
  ment and unforgiveness, and gives us insight
  and new ideas.

- **Zadkiel** (pronounced "ZAD-kee-el"). His
  name means "Righteousness of God," and
  he heals memory and mental functioning

In addition to calling upon the angels and archangels, you
may wish to invoke the power and assistance of the ascended
masters. These beings are great humans who help us from the
spirit world, and many of them are legendary teachers and
healers of various religions and cultures, such as Jesus,
Moses, Buddha, Quan Yin, Ganesh, the saints, and the goddesses. You'll also likely meet some ascended masters who

come to you during your crystal-therapy sessions. For more information, please refer to Doreen's book, *Archangels & Ascended Masters* (Hay House, 2003).

❈

Once you've called upon your angels and archangels (and, possibly, the ascended masters), they'll pulsate and stream the vast Divine love and light through you. Your crystal will concentrate and conduct this energy into whomever or whatever you're healing. For instance, if you're helping someone heal from grief, your angels may guide you to hold obsidian, lapis lazuli, or rose quartz near their heart chakra to ease feelings of loss or sorrow. Then the angels will send a huge wave of loving light through you and the crystal to clear the person's heart of depression, guilt, anger, or other blocking emotions. You and the stone will function together like a steam-cleaning hose at a car wash, sending powerful jets of cleansing light to release toxic energies.

Crystal-Therapy Forms

Crystal therapy takes many different forms, and the common thread is that crystals are tools that amplify your intentions to heal. Here are some ways that you may choose to use them:

- **Angelic Communication:** Hold (or meditate near) celestite and angelite, coupled with your intention to communicate with your guardian angels and archangels. Of course, crystals aren't required in order to hear and talk with angels. However, these particular stones are so attuned to the angelic realm that they act like megaphones, turning up the volume on your conversations with Heaven.

- **Astral Travel:** In astral or out-of-body travel, your soul soars freely throughout the Universe while safely attached to your body by a Divine silver cord. Holding or wearing apophyllite while meditating on your intention to make this journey can jump-start and enhance the experience.

- **Chakra Balancing:** Chakras are the major energy centers in our bodies, regulating physical vitality, emotional moods, and spiritual abilities. When these centers are balanced, we move through life in harmony;

when unbalanced, chaos appears in the related area. Crystals can help us clear and equalize our chakras. You can do this by lying down and placing the following stones on your body's chakra points, or by placing them beneath the bed or massage table underneath your reclining body. Another way is to simply hold and meditate upon each stone.

Chakra Location	Corresponding Crystals
Root (base of the spine)	Garnet, Smoky Quartz, Hematite
Sacral (between the tailbone and the navel)	Amber, Citrine, Orange Calcite
Solar Plexus (stomach area)	Tiger's-Eye, Citrine, Topaz
Heart (chest area)	Rose Quartz, Emerald, Kunzite

Throat (Adam's-apple area)	Aquamarine, Turquoise
Third Eye (between the eyes)	Amethyst, Lapis Lazuli
Ear (above the eyebrows)	Rutilated Quartz, Pink Tourmaline, Tanzanite
Crown (top of the head)	Sugilite, Clear Quartz, Charoite

- **Color Therapy:** Colored stones contain many of the same traits associated with color therapy, which normally includes tinted light or small bottles of dual-colored liquids, as in Aura-Soma (the therapy combining the healing energies of colors, plants, and crystals). Selecting representative stones allows for an increased ability to intensify or balance life. For example, a ruby reflects life-giving red energy, similar to blood flowing with ease throughout body. Rose quartz represents unconditional love, which corresponds with the vibration of the harmonious, universal love felt with pink.

- **Crystal Baths:** Acting as a cleansing agent, salt and mineral baths help keep the auric field clean by removing the residue of old or unwanted energy. You can put your crystals into the bathtub while you soak to boost the healing properties of the bathwater. Select the one associated with your desired intention (such as tangerine quartz to enhance creativity) using the chart in Chapter 7 of this book. Sea-salt baths and crystals work especially well in partnership with flower essences. However, try to select stones that are sturdy enough for salt water (or test them out first—for example, selenite, a type of gypsum, will melt under these conditions). Also note that stones can be placed on a dry spot near the bath, and their beneficial effects and energy exchange will still occur.

- **Drinking Water:** Adding clean and polished crystals to drinking water will help elevate the liquid's vibration while intensifying its healing aspects. *(Note: Caution should be used to avoid swallowing any stones.)*

- **Elixirs:** Adding powdered crystals to water creates a potent elixir. This ancient medicinal tool demands extensive knowledge to ensure that appropriate stones are used in the liquid, since the mineral kingdom contains numerous combinations of chemicals. Ingesting any mixture requires a sound understanding of the probable and potential effects on the physical body. For this reason, we recommend that you work with a certified practitioner, such as a homeopathic physician or a nutritionist, rather than creating elixirs unsupervised.

- **Feng Shui:** Feng Shui is the ancient Chinese art of placement, in which everything in our environment has meaning and purpose. Crystals are natural earthly elements that are often included in the intricate balancing of chi (energy) within homes and buildings. Crystals that correspond to the Feng Shui Bagua Map are listed on page 185 in this book.

- **Grounding and Protection:** If you feel spaced-out, as if you're wandering in a dreamlike state, you can use crystals to help ground you and recover your focus on the here-and-now. They can also increase and strengthen your personal energy shield so that you won't be bombarded by the world's intense and sometimes harsh energies. Hematite, black tourmaline, and obsidian are excellent touchstones when you're feeling despondent or out of sorts, or need to increase your personal energy shield. Carry them with you as quiet companions that will keep you down-to-earth.

- **Group Dynamics:** Cluster-formation quartz crystals (single crystals that have many individual points protruding from them like a starburst) bring harmony, cooperation, and efficiency to family and business meetings. Just as a group is composed of unique per-spectives, a cluster consists of individual points living as one. Set them near the meeting place, or wherever there's group communication.

- **Healing:** As has been discussed throughout this book so far, crystalline energy is an amazing ally when strengthening and repairing areas of imbalance or disease in all the bodies: etheric, emotional, and physical. Working with intention, heavenly guidance, and selected stones (such as those listed in Chapter 7), a commanding connection is created as a channel of loving energy flows from Heaven and Earth through the body.

- **Jewelry:** Wearing stones is very helpful, especially in the heart and throat areas. In this way, belts can add a new dimension by establishing a solid transmission near the solar plexus, while specific crystals can be used as adornments and healing tools as needed. The selection is best when made according to your planned activities and feelings that day (emotional associations can be found in Chapter 7).

- **Life Purpose:** Identifying and clarifying life-path issues is a common theme among our clients. One of the most effective stones for this topic is clear quartz used in conjunction with black tourmaline. This combination helps amplify intention and direction and aids in defining goals. Meditate while either holding the stones or sitting near them. Maintain the intention of receiving clear directions about your life purpose, and ask the stones to amplify your receptivity to this guidance.

- **Laying On of Stones:** Crystal healing frequently involves the application of specific crystals to the physical body in order to assist in the mending process. Several techniques for preventive and regenerative clearing are available. They're usually performed in partnership with a certified practitioner, who will use intuitive placement as well as standard layouts. Judith says, "Many of my clients need assistance to heal their emotional pain. One of the best methods is to lay a circle of rose quartz crystals on the chest, which helps them remember to integrate Divine love through crystal-energy channels."

- **Meditation:** Selecting and using crystals as meditation companions can be a tremendous energy accelerator. Using a double-terminated

(points on both ends) clear quartz crystal can
help increase the flow of Divine energy moving in and out of your being on all levels.

- **Personal Development:** Everyone has areas
  of potential improvement or development.
  Working with a corresponding stone speeds
  the progress while deepening the healing
  experience. For example, citrine builds confidence, fluorite deepens spiritual connection, and amethyst enhances clairvoyance.
  You can receive these benefits by holding the
  crystals, wearing them, meditating upon
  them, or a combination of all these methods.

- **Touchstones:** Carrying stones in your hand
  allows the crystal vibration to flow consis-
  tently through your energy field, using touch
  to access this soothing presence. Touchstones
  can help you stay focused on the present
  moment, while eliminating fear and accentu-
  ating the positive.

CHAPTER FOUR

CRYSTAL CARE AND SELECTION

We don't become "owners" of crystals, we become "guardians," in much the same way that we're guardians of our children and pets. When we live, sleep, heal, and work with these stones, we become aware of their lively and communicative energy. They're companions who speak to us on the deepest and most intuitive levels, which sensitive people can hear and understand.

Never underestimate the power of crystals, as Judith explains: "Here's one of my favorite illustrations of this point: A client took home a smoky quartz crystal, and I warned her that change would be fast-paced as she worked with her new 'friend.' Two weeks later, she returned chagrined and excited as her entire life began to shift in every area, from career to relationships. After a quiet discussion between her and the stone, it was decided that the stone would rest; so she covered it in silk, placed it inside a cabinet, and abstained from interacting with it for two weeks. When she began working with the crystal again, she learned how to monitor her ability to accept and integrate change, and got great results—the manifestation of her dreams with a business success and a new relationship."

Crystal Selection

Guardianship begins with the desire to make new friends with the mineral companions you select, and then being available and responsive to the relationship's bond. With this intention, crystals will come to live with you in the most surprising ways—people may give them to you as gifts, you may find them yourself, or *they* may find *you* through ingenious methods.

In addition to receiving stones through synchronicity, you can also shop for them: Crystals are sold at most metaphysical and New Age shops, health-food markets, crystal stores, and in some interior decorating and gift boutiques. Make sure that each piece is naturally formed (as opposed to human-made) using the methods described on page 16. Those labeled "Austrian," "Lead Crystal," or "Swarovski" are lovely as decorations or jewelry, but they lack the natural channeling abilities required for this therapy.

Use your sixth sense to help you make your selection by tuning in to the stone and allowing it to choose you. You may experience a feeling of "recognition" with one that calls to you, as though reconnecting to a member of your soul family; or you may need to touch, hold, see, or hear many of the crystals before making your selection. Take your time, just as you would when connecting with a potential family pet.

Here's another way to use your intuition when shopping for a crystal: Begin by holding it in your nondominant hand (the one you don't normally write with), since it receives the strongest energy signals. Then, close your eyes, and feel the stone's power. Next, point it toward your third eye (the very sensitive area between your two physical eyes), and run the tip down to your heart. If the crystal is charged and alive with healing energy and spirit, you'll feel a magnetic rush pushing against your third eye and heart. If you don't feel anything, it could mean that your sensitivity is temporarily diminished or that the stone's energy is low or clogged. You can always reactivate it, but why not shop for one with an energetic spirit?

Don't be surprised if the crystal you select isn't the clearest, largest, or most colorful—its beauty may not be immediately apparent to the physical eye. Just trust your intuition to guide you to the perfect choice, because waiting within the crystal is a loving, powerful ally and a wise friend; and as in any relationship, you'll *know* when you find the one that's right for you.

Crystal Cleansing

After you bring your new companion home, it's a good idea to cleanse it in order to release any old, toxic energies that it may have absorbed. The process will also help the two of you bond, and it will imbue the stone with your personal energy. Choosing how and when a crystal needs cleansing is a personal decision, as is the time required for clearing, but you'll know it's time when the stone's effectiveness seems to diminish, or when its energy feels "tired." Keep in mind that minerals used in a therapeutic practice should be cleansed after each client to release any energy residue.

There are several ways to purify crystals, including placing them in sea salt or in a natural water source (such as the ocean, a pond, or a stream); burying them in the earth; infusing them with sunlight or moonlight; or using prana by setting your intention to clean and blowing healing breath into the stone three times. *(**Note:** Some crystals, such as selenite* *and desert rose, will melt when placed in water. Others, such as amethyst or fluorite, will fade when placed in direct sunlight. Be sure to check for special conditions before choosing a cleansing process.)*

Crystal Programming and Charging

As discussed in the previous chapter, working with crystals requires, well, crystal clear intention. So ask yourself if you want to access information, receive or send healing vibrations, or connect with ascended masters. Or do you have something else in mind?

Crystals direct, amplify, and accelerate energy patterns, and they combine the strength of your desires with their individual gifts to assist you in the manifestation process. Once you've clarified your intentions, communicate with the stones through meditation, envisioning the healing purpose and practice you desire. When you clearly express your objective, mineral miracles will follow as the crystals absorb this intention into their essence and being . . . but rest assured that this programming can be changed or updated as required.

Remember that you can reenergize and recharge your companions by placing them in sunlight (with some exceptions) or moonlight. Doreen explains, "My research on

Atlantis and Babylon taught me that the evening prior to the full moon is an ideal time to charge your crystals with healing and magical energy."

Other Crystal Considerations: Placement, Travel, and Passing Them On

Your crystals will guide you in selecting their placement in your home or office through a tugging sensation, or even through a voice directing you to a certain place in a specific room. Trust your intuition—it's part of your energetic connection to the stones, which knows where they can be of most service to you and where they'll be happy. Visit often, and give them tender, loving care such as dusting, clearing, and regular recharging.

Once you've found locations for your crystals, you may want to place them on small velvet pillows, clear Lucite holders, or some other setting that signifies your respect and appreciation for them and their beauty. However, these new friends will look beautiful wherever they are, so don't worry if you don't have a special display for them.

Although they have a place at home, don't be surprised if you feel the urge to take your mineral companions with you when you travel. Having them on the road with you is a blessing, and you'll find that they keep the energy of hotel rooms high and clean. Before you leave, pack them in protective wrapping: Silk, velvet, or natural fibers are favorites; and leather is often used in the Native American tradition. You can ask your stones what type of wrapping they prefer.

Doreen travels extensively and takes her crystals in carry-ons (rather than checked luggage) because the delicate formations could become damaged by vigorous baggage handlers; and since she considers crystals to be alive, she wants to treat them with consideration. She says, "More than once, though, I've been stopped by airport security officers as they scan the crystal wands in my carry-on luggage. I usually find that they're genuinely curious about crystals, and a couple of them even asked me to do healing and manifestation treatments on them right there in the airport! Of course, I happily obliged."

Even though you handle and pack your crystals carefully, stones can shatter and points can break off at home as well as while traveling—this is just the course of nature. When the moment comes and you're faced with a "broken" stone, ask for guidance: Is it time for it to be reburied in the garden or in a houseplant; or to be given to the ocean, a lake, or a stream? Has a new touchstone been given to you? As you become familiar with the language of crystal energy, the new direction will become clear—but most important, trust your intuition and personal guidance.

You may also receive intuitive guidance to give a particular stone to a specific person as a gift. When this happens, know that the crystal's work with you is complete—it's been "reassigned" a new task helping someone else, so pass it along as you're guided, with faith and knowledge that you're bringing great blessings to the crystal and its new human guardian.

Now that you have a strong sense of the emotional components involved in working with crystals, let's look at some of the technical aspects of crystal therapy.

CHAPTER FIVE

ON <u>PHANTOMS,</u> AND OTHER QUARTZ TERMINOLOGY

Quartz crystal is a powerful and exciting stone for personal use and healing work. This natural energy conductor is the top choice in electronics and watches, and it also makes up the prismatic points on wizards' scepters and magical wands (which may be why it's associated with mysticism). Adding to this reputation, experienced crystal practitioners use jargon to describe the various characteristics of this stone—terms such as *windows, record keepers,* and *rutilated.* We'd like to explain some of this terminology in order to deepen your understanding and appreciation of the quartz crystal's gifts—which can take your healing work to new levels. The following chart will assist you in understanding these words, as well as help you recognize the characteristics in your own stones:

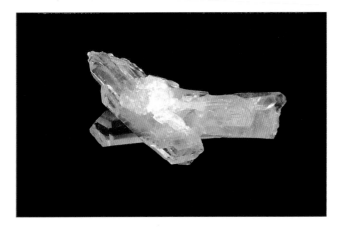

Formation Name: Bridge

Characteristic: A small crystal attached to a larger one, similar to an incomplete cross

Attribute: The small crystal bridges the inner and outer worlds to create a channel of wisdom

Formation Name: Channeling

Characteristics: Seven-sided face on the stone's front with a perfect triangle on the back

Attributes: Channeling accesses the source of wisdom from ascended masters or personal guides; this feature also eases communication and enhances learning

Formation Name: Cluster

Characteristic: Multiple terminations
or points from a single base

Attribute: A cluster is good for group energy—
it's an excellent team stone

Formation Name: Crystal Ball

Characteristic: Human-made sphere; it can be all-natural quartz or fused (reconstituted crystals forged through heat and shaped into a sphere)

Attribute: This familiar shape rounds out group communication and is also useful for reviewing the past and looking into the future

Formation Name: Double Terminated

Characteristic: Points at both ends of the stone

Attribute: A double-terminated formation completes the energy-flow integration both in and out of the person working with it

Formation Name: Generator

Characteristic: Six faces terminating in a single point

Attribute: This powerful energy tool is a wonderful meditation partner that supplies a feeling of strength

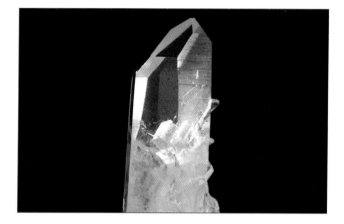

Formation Name: In and Out

Characteristic: Small crystal protrudes from, or into, the main body

Attribute: Use this stone when you need help bridging the gap between different spiritual dimensions or in finding your inner self

Formation Name: Laser Wand

Characteristic: Slender, tapered crystal

Attribute: A wand accelerates communication with your inner self and cuts through energetic residue—it's an excellent healing tool

Formation Name: Left-Handed

Characteristic: Extra facet on left side
of the stone (when facing it)

Attribute: This formation draws out negative energy
and enhances right-brain activities such as creativity
and visualization

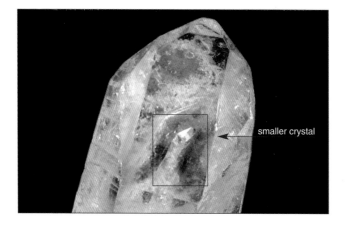

smaller crystal

Formation Name: Manifestation

Characteristic: Small crystal completely enclosed in a larger one

Attribute: As its name suggests, this actualization tool helps manifest goals into reality

Formation Name: Phantom

Characteristic: Pyramid reflection within a stone that's often referred to as a "ghost crystal"

Attribute: You can intensify your universal awareness and help unlock past lives with the phantom, for it links to the Higher Self's wisdom

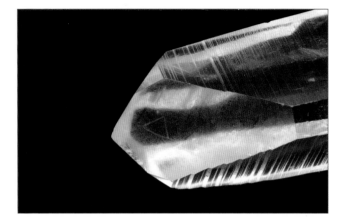

Formation Name: Record Keeper

Characteristic: Naturally etched triangle(s) usually found on one or more of the crystal's faces

Attribute: Acting as a tool to access ancient wisdom, a record keeper helps you understand and receive personal lessons in life's patterns (and release old habits)

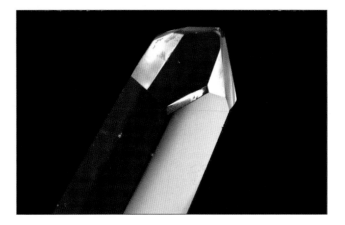

Formation Name: Right-Handed

Characteristic: Extra facet on the right side of a crystal (when facing it)

Attribute: This formation enhances left-brain activities such as analytical capabilities and traditional problem solving

Formation Name: Rutilated (Angel Hair) and Tourmalated

Characteristics: Linear inclusions found in quartz; usually black, red-brown, or yellow (metallic) mineral deposits

Attribute: The addition of a foreign element into the main stone brings two levels of energy to bear on the focus of your intention—for example, the actual characteristics of quartz are blended with the grounding strength of a tourmaline inclusion, amplifying the power of both.

Formation Name: Soul mate

Characteristic: Twin crystals of similar size on a single base

Attribute: This pair helps you recognize your soul mate or "soul family"

Formation Name: Time Link

Characteristic: Window near the point shaped like a parallelogram (a four-sided figure with opposite sides parallel and of equal length)

Attribute: A time link enhances communication among all levels of the self

Formation Name: Window

Characteristic: A diamond face centered
on the front of the facets or points

Attribute: This is a window to internal truths,
and a symbol of Heaven and Earth meeting

CHAPTER SIX
CRYSTAL GRIDS

If you've ever watched a large building's construction, you've seen the steel framework that supports the final structure, which is known as a *grid*. In a similar way, you can construct an energetic grid to support whatever intention or healing goal you desire. Instead of using steel beams, you'll place crystals in specific locations so that the energy from each stone will form a support system that's palpable and clairvoyantly visible to those who are sensitive and attuned. Yet even if you can't see or feel the power, this is a dynamic method of crystal therapy with noticeable results.

Grids are created for many personal and global reasons, and quartz points are the stones most often used in these beautiful prayer mandalas. In this chapter, we've included some suggestions for specific situations, but don't be afraid to experiment with various crystals and your own vision. Forming these patterns is similar to any creative venture (such as cooking). While you may initially follow a recipe, you'll eventually shift the ingredients to suit your own tastes. Once the shape is complete, you can then meditate with intention to activate and accelerate its energy, just as your ancestors have done through the ages.

Creating a Crystal Grid

Grids are an ancient, time-honored way to contain and build the power of prayer and healing energy. For centuries, people have joined with nature in order to link with the eternal wisdom of Heaven, leaving us familiar images such as Stonehenge in England; the French Carnac stones; and ancient temples and pyramids in Egypt, Greece, Mexico, Hawaii, and South America.

These powerful networks hold the memories and energy patterns from many ceremonies of intent. Even today, as you walk through the ancient stone circles and temples, the current surrounds you in powerful ways. This force comes partly from the intensified electromagnetic field of the stone configurations, and partly from the lingering vibration of past prayers for individual and communal harmony.

As Judith elaborates, "Many of my private clients are searching for an elusive sense of peace in some area of life, and they often ask about implementing crystal energy to help manifest a desired state, such as finding a soul mate, identifying their life purpose, or attaining abundance. Partnering with the mineral kingdom using a grid system is simply another way to help recognize and activate universal flow."

Since crystal grids are geometric forms that facilitate an energetic flow using stones and patterns, they're similar to focusing your meditation through a mandala, a labyrinth, or a pyramid. The stones used for the framework may be raw (natural state), tumbled or polished (machine finished), or faceted (machine cut); and the pattern may be as simple as four pieces of rose quartz placed in your bedroom's corners to enhance love, or it may be more complex sacred geometry to accelerate spiritual ascension. Whether your grid addresses a simple need (such as a better night's sleep) or something more intricate, it simply requires your clear intention, trust, and commitment for you to receive the full benefit.

When connecting with the mineral kingdom using this format, you're asking to create a unified field of power in which thoughts and desires manifest, because stones that are placed in a particular shape—especially quartz points—heighten energetic vibrations and movement. As an extra support, you can request that angels join you in the process, since they purify your intentions and take them to a higher level, which leads to harmonious changes and healings.

Nine Steps to the Grid

1. **Determine Its Intention.** You can build a grid to help support any goal, intention, or desire, so your first step is deciding, "What is it for?" Since it will amplify your feelings, thoughts, and intentions, it's crucial that you have a very clear focus. If you have any fears, doubts, guilt, or other emotions that could potentially disrupt your desired outcome, just call upon Archangel Jophiel to help you attain a positive outlook.

2. **Decide on the Size.** Selecting the appropriate size is up to you. A grid that's small enough to set on a tray can be just as powerful as one that's large enough to welcome a body in the center, since using the stones as a meditation focus point sufficiently expands their energy. However, there are times when the best choice is sitting inside a larger formation to feel its vibrations.

3. **Find a Location.** Sometimes the locale for your grid will be obvious (such as the bedroom when you want to sleep better), but at other times, convenience is the deciding factor. For example, placing the pattern in your personal meditation space would help ensure that other people don't move your crystals or disrupt you while you're focusing on them. For more options, remember that you can also build outdoors, just as our ancestors did.

4. **Use Feng Shui.** As an optional enhancement to further clarify your pattern's intention, use the "Feng Shui magic square" (nine defined areas), called the *Bagua Map,* to help choose a location. For example, if you want to improve your love life, create a grid in your bedroom's Relationship area and meditate there on a regular basis—the results can be exceptional! We've included information about the Bagua Map on page 183 of this book.

5. **Clear the Space.** Once you determine the intent, size, and location of your project, you'll need to purify and lift the energy in that spot. Any space-clearing method will

work, such as burning sage, placing bowls of sea salt in the room, calling upon Archangel Michael, ringing a bell, and the like.

6. **Create Ambience.** Music, candles, and incense all add to the sense of tranquility and peace in the sacred space that you've decided to use.

7. **Place the Crystals.** Either using the recommendations in this chapter or following your own guidance, place the crystals around your chosen location. If you're using quartz, face all the stones in the same direction to heighten their energy flow: The points go to the right to send energy outward, and they go to the left to receive energy. Don't worry—as long as you're following your inner guidance, you can't make a mistake in the building process.

8. **Meditate and Empower the Grid.** Sit quietly, either next to the crystals or in the center of the pattern, and visualize lines of energy connecting each stone above and around you. You may see various lines,

shapes, and colors; and hear celestial music or whirring sounds, which are all displays of the converging power.

9. **Listen.** Focus on your breath in order to quiet your mind, and then pay attention to any ideas, visions, words, or feelings that come to you. Surrender any distracting thoughts or worries to the angels so that you can visualize your desire as already being complete, and feel gratitude that this is so. Thank the Universe for its ever-flowing abundance, asking the angels to help you be open and receive, and then complete the meditation by saying positive affirmations such as the ones outlined on the following pages.

Each time you build and use a crystal grid, you'll develop a greater awareness of its energy and power—so relax into the process and have fun! To help you get started, we've outlined some common crystal combinations for frequently requested areas of focus, plus affirmations to assist you in manifesting your dreams.

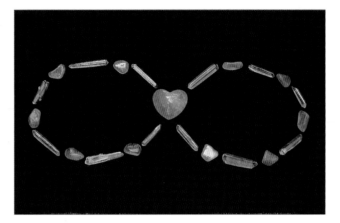

LOVE/ROMANCE GRID

Abundance

Crystals: 8 clear quartz points
and 3 pieces of jade or citrine

Shape: Lay out a circle of quartz points with the jade or
citrine outlining a triangle shape in the center. This pattern
functions best when placed in the Feng Shui Wealth
area of a home or business.

Affirmation: Abundance in all forms now
flows to me with Divine grace.

Angelic Communication

Crystals: 9 clear quartz points and
2 pieces of angelite or celestite

Shape: Form a triangle using the nine pieces of quartz
(three pieces on each side of the triangle), and place the
angelite or celestite stones in the center, touching each
other. This works well in the Partnership with
Helpful People area of the home.

Affirmation: I now fully accept the wisdom,
insight, and protection of my angels.

Creativity

Crystals: 7 quartz points and
11 pieces of carnelian

Shape: Alternate the stones to create a spiral. This grid
is an excellent addition to the Creativity area of a home,
studio, or office, since it helps the movement
of thought into form.

Affirmation: I feel and express the creative
spirit within me now.

Forgiveness

Crystals: 8 pieces of rose quartz, 4 pieces of aventurine,
2 pieces of moonstone, and 2 pieces of hematite

Shape: Make a double circle with an outside ring of rose
quartz and an inner ring with a mix of aventurine and
moonstone, putting the hematite in the center.
It's often most helpful to place these stones
in the Self-Knowledge area.

Affirmation: The unconditional love of Heaven now fills me with love, compassion, and understanding.

Harmony

Crystals: 6 pieces of rose quartz and 12 amethyst points

Shape: Alternate the stones to form a heart shape that can go in any of the Bagua-Map sectors to increase feelings of peace, serenity, and unconditional love.

Affirmation: My life is in Divine order, and I now move in harmony with the Universe.

Health/Healing

Crystals: 11 pieces of rose quartz or moonstone, 11 pieces of malachite, and 11 pieces of turquoise

Shape: Arrange the stones in three interconnecting circles, representing mind, body, and spirit. This design is perfect for the Health area, since it will activate positive flow in the body's systems.

Affirmation: I enjoy perfect, robust,
and joyful health now.

Life Purpose/Career

Crystals: 1 quartz cluster, 12 pieces of black
tourmaline, and 12 pieces of citrine

Shape: Alternate the tourmaline and citrine to create
a double diamond, and place the quartz point in the
center. Keep the grid at your office or in the Career
area at home in order to facilitate awareness and
acceptance of your life mission, while asking
for support from the community.

Affirmation: I now know, accept, and act
in accordance with my Divine purpose.

Love/Romance

Crystals: 12 quartz points, 10 pieces of rose quartz,
and 1 heart-shaped rose quartz

Shape: Make a figure eight (which is an infinity symbol), and alternate the stones and points to signify the union of male and female energies (these energies are also part of same-sex relationships). Place the rose quartz heart in the center point of the figure eight to symbolize the one love joining the two souls. This layout works perfectly for the Relationship corner of your home, or in your bedroom.

Affirmation: I am now in perfect alignment with love on all levels.

Protection

Crystals: 5 quartz points and 12 pieces of black or rainbow obsidian

Shape: Create a square using the obsidian, placing the quartz points together in a star formation in the center of the square. This grid can be placed in any area of the Feng Shui map related to your life area of concern (e.g., financial protection would mean placing the crystals in the Wealth section of your home).

Affirmation: I release fear, knowing that I am fully loved and protected by Heaven, now and forever.

Sleep

Crystals: 4 pieces of rose quartz and
1 piece of rainbow obsidian or hematite

Shape: Put one piece of rose quartz in each corner
of the bedroom with the obsidian or hematite under the
bed to create an atmosphere of love and
security that will improve your sleep.

Affirmation: I am loved and protected.
It is now safe to relax and sleep.

World Peace

Crystals: 24 quartz points and 1 malachite and azurite sphere (a stone of the same combination will also work)

Shape: Make a circle of 12 quartz points with the malachite and azurite in the center; then add four lines of 3 quartz points each, which symbolize the four directions: north, south, east, and west. Place the grid in the Self-Knowledge Feng Shui area to buoy faith and inner peace.

Affirmation: The world is in perfect and Divine harmony now.

Chapter Seven

A Directory of Crystals, Their Healing Properties, and Their Messages

Each type of crystal has a specific healing purpose and specialty, from physical health to emotional support; and their colors, shapes, and other characteristics determine which life areas they're best suited to help restore. On the following pages, you'll read descriptions of the major crystal groups we've selected, which are readily available and easy to find, and which act as powerful allies in conducting healing work.

You'll find a photo of the mineral and its variations; a pronunciation guide for the more unusual terms; a summary of each mineral's healing properties; the archangels to call upon when working with that particular stone (keeping in mind that you can always appeal to other angels and ascended masters as you feel guided); and a channeled message from each crystal group and variety—every one of which was given and received with love, respect, and integrity. May the crystals and their words assist you on your journey!

❀

Mineral Name: Agate

Pronunciation: "AG-it"

Archangels: Michael and Raziel

Colors: Combinations of brown, blue, gray, green, orange, red, and white

Healing Properties: Agate strengthens the mind and body, helps you discern the truth, and is a powerful healing stone when it's used in conjunction with the chakra color system. You can do this by selecting the agate color that corresponds with each energy center (red for root, orange for sacral, yellow for solar plexus, green for heart, light blue for throat, dark blue for third eye, violet for ears, and purple for crown).

Message: "The rivers of time immemorial circulate in the patterns of my being; and within my form, shadows dance in swirling movements, happily mixing colors, as though capturing a vision of ribbons moving upon the wind, framing an endless sky.

"Those who enter my space of antiquity will find wisdom, confidence, and perspicuity. Ask us to assist, and without fail, one of us will step forward. Cousins abound in my clan, each unique, yet aligned with the power and strength of the earth elements. These members of my group share a personal perspective enriched by their experience and understanding, just as in your family. Take time to look at your relationships with eyes of compassion, asking that others share their history with you. Learn with an open heart."

Agate Variations

Blue Lace Agate

Archangel: Raguel

Colors: Sky blue and white patterning, reminiscent of intricate filigree

Healing Properties: This variety facilitates serenity, creating a sense of self-awareness that helps maintain balance during times of stress.

Message: "Calming in nature, I act as a buffer for sensitive individuals by keeping the chaos of daily activities at bay while establishing a peaceful environment within the self."

Botswana Agate

Archangels: Raguel and Chamuel

Colors: Light blue and gray swirls

Healing Properties: Peaceful movements of blue and gray help soothe your nerves, lift depression, and focus your thoughts on service.

Message: "The world extends in scope and beauty as you open in awareness. I'll help you release the burden of depression and despair so that you can look beyond yourself in moments of sorrow. Have faith—the Universe is a joyous place founded in love and based in harmony."

Crazy Lace Agate

Archangel: Ariel

Color: A delicate "lace" pattern on agate

Healing Properties: This is an exceptional tool for reconnecting to Mother Earth, and it adds a feeling of "groundedness" when multiple priorities demand your attention.

Message: "By blending Earth colors, I bring a balanced understanding of the physical realm, which translates into body attunement for those feeling ungrounded. Sit with me in contemplation to reestablish a sense of wholeness and well-being."

Fire Agate

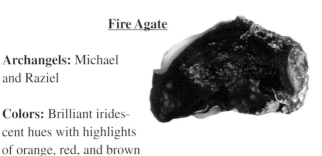

Archangels: Michael and Raziel

Colors: Brilliant iridescent hues with highlights of orange, red, and brown

Healing Properties: This is the stone of the astrologer, which also instills a sense of safety and protection.

Message: "Use me to unlock feelings of trust and safety. Know that all is well in the world as fire, water, air, and earth combine in the wheel of understanding as they do in astrology."

Green Moss Agate

Archangels: Raphael, Ariel, and Uriel

Color: A touch of green in a mosslike formation of clear, white stone

Healing Properties: A symbol of nature incarnate, this stone is an excellent partner for members of the elemental realm. When used as a touchstone, it helps create an immediate bond with Mother Earth.

Message: "Renew your connection with nature when you gaze into me, for I reflect the refreshment found in solitude while walking in the woods. Ever peaceful, touch me to feel the centeredness of Mother Earth and bring that feeling of serene power into your life."

Mineral Name: Amber

Archangel:
Ariel and Jeremiel

Colors: Translucent tones
of brown and yellow

Healing Properties: Amber is an ancient manifestation
tool that can help you attain your goals when you use it
with focused intention.

Message: "I'm one of the oldest known adornments, for
human eyes are attracted to the luminosity of my color
and cool texture. I've often been used in trade as people
moved around the globe, providing a source of income
along with soothing energy to those who journey with me.

"As fossilized resin, I mix the remnants of sweetness
from the plant kingdom with captured artifacts of nature
that reflect the blending of the plant, animal, and mineral
realms. I'm a tool for earthly manifestation and a reminder to honor environmental needs. Best used in jewelry,
I act as a balancing agent for yin and yang energies."

Mineral Name:
Amethyst

Archangel: Michael

Colors: Lavender to
deep purple

Healing Properties:
This calming, protective stone is an excellent meditation
tool that accelerates the development of psychic abilities.

Message: "Link to the Divine by using the frequencies
of my vibrational ladder. Through heightened awareness,
I assist in quieting internal chatter so that you can
acknowledge the peace of oneness. If you're interested
in expansion, I'll train your intuition by accelerating the
opening of your chakras so that you can receive and
integrate universal wisdom and transcend established
boundaries.

"As a key to the self, I unlock the perfection that
can be hidden by personality, and thus reveal the glow-
ing intelligence of your soul. It's my gift to accentuate
the positive aspects of your being in order to bring forward etheric awareness with the knowledge that Heaven
is now available on Earth."

Mineral Name: Angelite

Pronunciation: "AN-gel-ite"

Archangels: Haniel and Raguel

Color: Creamy sky blue

Healing Properties: Angelite works to remove fears with calming energy that increases faith and serenity. It's also an exceptional stone for enhancing astral travel and angelic communication.

Message: "Dearest ones, know me as the voice of Heaven. Upon my vibration, prayers are carried unto the angels, where there's only love, completeness, and peace. I stand with you as a guardian of hope, a messenger of light, a teacher, and a friend. Support surrounds you, and there's no separation other than that which you choose to experience. If you're feeling a sense of lack, look within to see what belief can be brought forward for review and realignment. Quiet yourself in meditation with me so that you can receive blessings of wisdom. Angels whisper softly . . . will you listen? Or will you wait to feel what cannot be ignored?"

Mineral Name:
Apophyllite

Pronunciation:
"A-puh-FILE-ite"

Archangels:
Raziel and Haniel

Colors: Clear, green,
peach, and white natural pyramid shapes

Healing Properties: This crystal enhances clairvoyance
and assists out-of-body travel. In addition, it's an outstanding meditation stone that links with angelic energy
and helps you remember your dreams.

Message: "Enter my vibrational chamber prepared to
travel, as I'm the wizard of momentum between dimensions. I play the role of protective escort as you visit new
planes of existence and travel in this world without your
physical vessel. Practice losing the intimidation of form,
and shift your awareness to the subtle transmission of
energetic expansion. Feel the intensity of my pulse as I
lie centered in your palms, and imagine a freedom from
the corporeal realm combined with complete awareness.
Bilocation, astral travel—the masters have proven these
possibilities to you. The future is now."

Mineral Name:
Aquamarine

Archangels:
Ariel and Raguel

Colors: Translucent
sea-foam green to pale blue

Healing Properties: Aquamarine works to balance the
emotional, mental, and physical bodies, and it helps create
an awareness and integration of universal truths.

Message: "I unite with you to cleanse the environment
with dedication and fervor for our shared commitment to
keeping the waters of life pristine. Clear your aura with
me while synchronizing your physical, emotional, mental,
and etheric bodies. I augment composure, leaving hints of
fairies at play within your improved humor and disposi-
tion. Wear me close to your heart to feel the sea, recalling
dolphin dances with innocent childlike delight. Lose your
concerns in my ocean of green and blue, releasing fear
and anxiety to the Sea Goddesses and replacing your old
beliefs with blissful knowingness and trust."

Mineral Name:
Aventurine

Pronunciation:
"Av-EN-chu-reen"

Archangels:
Jophiel and Raguel

Colors: Creamy blue, brown, green, peach, red

Healing Properties: This stone heals heart pain and accelerates the balancing of yin and yang energy within you.

Message: "Employ me when learning to receive gifts in the authentic cycle of abundance and prosperity. Most often you are willing and expecting to give, yet you say *no* unconsciously when presented with opportunities to receive. Accepting all the ways abundance materializes is an integral part of participating in the natural flow. Remember that male (giving) and female (receiving) energies and characteristics are equally important. Just as day and night maintain equilibrium, so do yin and yang . . . and so must sharing and receiving be part of your daily practice. This process is the basis for healthy relationships with your family and friends, and it allows the Universe to care for you."

Mineral Name:
Azurite

Pronunciation:
"AZH-ur-ite"

Archangels:
Haniel, Raziel, and Zadkiel

Color: Brilliant dark blue

Healing Properties: Azurite is a transformation stone that's linked with creativity, intuition, inspiration, and eliminating illusion.

Message: "The rich hues of midnight skies are captured in my color, with sage advice lingering in my patterns. I bring the deep intuitive insight and wisdom of the feminine Divine. With me, truth is spoken, sure and strong. I won't tolerate deception, and I bring to light that which is no longer of service to you. Invite me into your life only when you're prepared to dissolve illusions and step forward into your full essence. Will you accept the transformation offered? Magician, will you walk forward and share your gifts? The world needs your healing grace this day."

Mineral Names:
Azurite and Malachite

Pronunciation:
"AZH-ur-ite;
MAL-uh-kite"

Archangels:
Ariel, Raguel, Raphael, and Zadkiel

Colors: Deep blue and green

Healing Properties: The powerful properties of these stones blend to create a new energy focused on accepting personal power while reducing stress.

Message: "Clearly, we're the earth, bound together in a timeless union of stone that reflects Heaven's view and combines our individual healing abilities and gifts. We bring awareness of the need for environmental cleansing of the pollution that stifles the world's resources and threatens the well-being of all. We stand ready to assist in creating a peaceful manifestation of the energetic forces we activate, so take us with you when you speak from your heart about the need for change.

"Respect our home, for it nurtures your very being, and gently cleanse your environment without harsh action or thoughts. As an individual, remove the chemicals from your home; as a community, focus on cleaning up industries, neighborhoods, parks, and water supplies. Simplify your days, recycle, reclaim water, and honor Mother Earth—as she honors you—in order to perpetuate the cycle of life.

"Internally, are your thoughts clear, or are they muddled by overwhelming stimulation from 'busyness'? Quiet yourself and allow yourself to surrender into spirit, so you may awaken as refreshed as when the earth is soothed by rain."

Mineral Name: Calcite

Archangels: Ariel, Azrael, Haniel, Michael, Raguel, Raphael, Raziel, Sandalphon, and Uriel

Colors: Cream, orange, blue, green, honey, brown, pink, and gray—with a somewhat soft, waxy complexion.

Healing Properties: With gentle strength, calcite provides a boost of energy to the foundational structure of the physical, mental, emotional, and spiritual bodies. It also helps with aura balancing.

Message: "We're a family of colors united as the people of the earth. Each of us is different at first glance, yet we're much the same upon deeper review. We carry the history of *being* within us: Shaped in the cradle of the earth by water and air, we bring emotions to light. Today we ask you to partake in a journey of exploration as brothers and sisters, with trust and understanding. Peel back the layers of emotional sediment to openly reveal your magical essence."

CALCITE VARIATIONS

Blue Calcite

Archangels: Jophiel, Raguel, and Raphael

Healing Properties: This blue stone helps ease joint pain and unlock the underlying reason for discomfort.

Message: "Speak of where the body is weary, holding tension or disease, so I may work with you to expel the negativity locked in your physical self. Journey with me in quiet contemplation, and I will reveal the point of pain, then help you acknowledge and release whatever doesn't support your highest good."

Brown Calcite

Archangels: Raguel and Uriel

Healing Properties: Brown calcite acts as a stabilizer when you're faced with conflicting priorities, so it's a wonderful stone for parents and businesspeople.

Message: "Grounding stabilization is my gift. Call on me when activities accelerate and you're overburdened, and I'll assist you with discretion and prioritization."

Creamy Calcite

Archangels: Azrael, Haniel, and Raziel

Color: Creamy yellow white

Healing Properties: As an emotional balancer, this crystal creates a sense of lightness and ease and assists with astral travel.

Message: "I lift the burdens from your soul as you move in synchronicity, traveling lightly into other spaces of time and awareness. Hold me and fly into the ether so that you may discover yourself in all ways."

Gray Calcite

Archangel: Michael

Healing Properties: The gray variety of this mineral establishes focus on being centered in your personal power and promotes clear thoughts that assist decision making.

Message: "I support you during change, guide your decisions, and help you reclaim personal power. Place me in your environment to shield and protect you, and know that you're a child of God, perfect and loved."

Green Calcite

Archangel: Raphael

Healing Properties: This is a wonderful healing stone for the physical body that brings Divine flow into your life with ease and harmony.

Message: "Feel the life force move through me as we connect in spirit. Rest your mind, and disengage from the voices chattering inside you—their negativity isn't authentic. You know the truth: The Universe is abundant, and you're safe, protected, and loved."

Honey Calcite

Archangels: Ariel and Raphael

Color: Light brown

Healing Properties: Honey calcite helps cleanse toxins and bring your body into alignment for optimal well-being.

Message: "Reduce the toxins in your environment with my help. Begin by looking around with critical awareness and removing those items that don't support your health in all areas. Since universal law abhors a vacuum, you're making space to receive appropriate replacements. Trust that you're opening yourself to new good."

Orange Calcite

Archangel: Sandalphon

Healing Properties: This crystal brings a fresh awareness and appreciation of creative expression, reminding you to embrace your own abilities.

Message: "Join with me in play. Remember the days you spent in idle contemplation of simple pleasures such as watching butterflies emerge from their cocoons, water rippling as stones skipped over it, and clouds drifting across the sky. You were fascinated and in awe. Hold me and look again with innocent eyes of wonder, allowing the perfection of your expression to emerge. Write, draw, dance, sing, compose, laugh, play . . . reveal the Divine within you."

Pink Calcite

Archangels: Ariel and Jophiel

Healing Properties: This pink stone clears and rebalances your heart chakra, which increases self-love while expanding your overall capacity for compassion.

Message: "Be gentle with yourself and allow quiet time for heart clearing, because as you love yourself, you're more able to love others. Give generously by nurturing your well-being, and in turn, you'll teach healing self-love to others."

Mineral Name:
Carnelian

Pronunciation:
"Car-NEEL-yun"

Archangel: Gabriel

Color: Translucent orange

Healing Properties: Carnelian creates a balance between mental focus and creative inspiration, allowing your vision to be actualized. Thus, it's a wonderful touchstone for creative people.

Message: "I'm the artists' stone, reflecting soulful expression through words and actions. I inspire intensity of movement in dance, and I lend fire to designers. In whatever manner it's sparked, I add a new dimension of depth to the creativity in your life, and I attract new people and experiences that support your vision. Those of you in the arts may wear me proudly, displaying your connection to the energy of the sacral chakra. It's your birthright to know the power of creativity, so choose to construct your life as you know it to be true: filled with unconditional love, clear purpose, abundance, and perfect health."

Mineral Name: Celestite

Pronunciation:
"SELL-ess-tite"

Archangels: Gabriel and Raguel

Color: Translucent blue

Healing Properties: This crystal assists with evolution to higher levels of consciousness and brings an awareness of personal truth. It also serves as a communication tool for linking with the angels.

Message: "As an angelic messenger, I'm a conduit expediting the vibration of prayers on this plane. Moving between dimensions, I help integrate levels of consciousness and escalate ascension into the domain of Heaven's grace. I'm found with those who accept that angels are here now, and I bring those with instinctive appreciation to a conscious initiation. Communication with the Divine is a birthright, and intuition or angelic guidance is available to everyone. It's a choice that defines aptitude, or attentiveness to subtle signs that create interaction.

"I'm also a stone of personal truth. Through working with me in meditation, doors will open: You'll see the essence of your Higher Self and learn how to bring forward all your gifts."

Mineral Name:
Charoite

Pronunciation:
"CHAR-o-ite"

Archangels:
Haniel, Michael, and Raziel

Colors: Dark lavender to blue purple with black-and-white veins

Healing Properties: This third-eye stone enhances psychic awareness and abilities and acts as a catalyst for discovering and healing hidden fears.

Message: "My name is a derivative of the word for *charming* or *magical* in the native language of my homeland, Russia. I've newly arrived to help the progressive evolution of humankind. Accelerate your clairvoyance by working with me to focus your attention and release the constrictions of your third eye. Confining beliefs and fears are identified and relinquished through my elevated vibration. Offering sage advice with quiet dignity, I'm a stone of the wise ones: Ever present and ever ready, I assist in divining truth."

Mineral Name:
Chrysanthemum Stone

Pronunciation:
"Krih-SAN-thuh-mum"

Archangel: Ariel

Colors: Grayish black with white imprints, similar to its flower namesake

Healing Properties: This is the stone of change. It expands compatibility, building unity through fun and innocence. In addition, it removes obstructions, and helps you start or continue moving toward your goals.

Message: "Expect the unexpected with me. For as an elemental takes pleasure in the mischief of change, so do I. (Perhaps that's why fairies peek out, showing their wings in my blossoms.) Change without pain is possible, and I'm here to prove it. Visualize what you want, and I will work with you. Don't be surprised if I add a little gift. Laughter is joy spoken out loud. Remember the curiosity you felt as a child? Nothing was unquestionable or unchangeable—that is still the truth. You created the change. What will it be?"

Mineral Name:
Chrysocolla

Pronunciation:
"Kris-OH-col-la"

Archangels: Azrael and Raguel

Colors: Light blue to blue green

Healing Properties: Chrysocolla balances your heart center, which brings stability and emotional awareness. It focuses the healing energy of universal love into your personal experience.

Message: "I arrived to help maintain human equilibrium during emotional eruptions. Joy is your natural state, yet there are times when sorrow prevails during the earthly experience. When you're confronted with emotional pain, I help you release feelings of separation and grief through quiet meditation. With me, you sense refreshing reminders of God's loving support in unexpected ways. Feelings of sadness fade as I share new perspectives through heart-healing vibrational patterns. I'm a splendid companion, whether encased in silver or simply tumbled and held in a pocket, a reminder that all is perfect in the ever-flowing river of life."

Mineral Name:
Chrysocolla and Malachite

Pronunciation:
"Kris-OH-col-la;
MAL-a-kite"

Archangel: Raguel

Colors: Combinations of light blue, blue green, and dark green, with swirls of pattern variations within the stone

Healing Properties: This composite is excellent for business. It helps you access abundance, increases your capacity to love, and assists you in breaking down barriers.

Message: "Businesspeople welcome me into their world, for they recognize that prosperity's foundation is service from the heart. In blended harmony, I facilitate an ever-increasing appreciation that business is about communities working together toward common goals. I'm an exceptional tool for unifying diverse groups, as I reflect the beauty of unique views merging to create an improved product. The combination of my attributes opens spirits to receive abundance in all forms. Keep me close at hand as you build bridges of peace."

Mineral Name:
Chrysoprase

Pronunciation:
"KRIS-uh-praze"

Archangel: Raphael

Colors: Apple green
to lemon

Healing Properties: This light, joyous stone works to heal personal problems and lift depression with calming, healing energy.

Message: "Joy is our intended state, so when you're feeling anything other than the brilliance of completeness within your being, it's a sign to rekindle the spark of unity. Hold me close to your heart and know that separation is but an illusion and that you're never alone. Feel the presence of love surrounding you at every moment—open your heart and eyes to sense it fully in your life. Interwoven in the tapestry of Divine design is the beauty of shared experiences and understanding. To find it, move out of your self-concern and into the space of service, and embrace the essence of exuberance."

Mineral Name:
Cinnabar

Pronunciation:
"SIH-nuh-bar"

Archangels:
Ariel and Raguel

Color: Red

Healing Properties: Often referred to as a *merchant stone,* cinnabar assists in creating profitable business transactions while establishing a sense of abundance.

Message: "Shining brilliantly within the boundaries of my black-and-white matrix, a glorious shade of life-giving red beckons to you. Merchants have recognized me for centuries as an unequaled partner in prosperity, and I've stood guard in treasure chests throughout world, clearing energy and inviting in the everlasting flow of wealth. I have a history of stimulating ideas, creativity, and action to develop labors of passion. By supporting ingenuity and resourcefulness in business acumen, I help you solve problems and develop supportive relationships. Invite me to work with you, and together we'll dissolve limiting beliefs and actualize sustained prosperity."

Mineral Name: Citrine

Pronunciation: "SIH-treen"

Archangels:
Ariel, Gabriel, and Uriel

Colors: Yellow to
deep golden brown

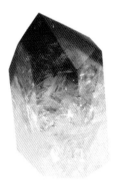

Healing Properties: This crystal increases self-esteem and is a powerful alignment tool that works with the Higher Self to heal old patterns and attract abundance.

Message: "Magic wells of golden light within me reflect universal perfection, similar to the Christ light. I add to your realization of universal flow, and when I'm used with focused intent, your visualizations are fulfilled in glory. The miraculous abundance of the Universe manifests without hesitation when you recognize that your thoughts are currency. I facilitate this energy exchange, which is why I'm known as a merchant stone. You see, abundance isn't only money—it's also health, time, and relationships, all of which enrich the manifestation of your life-supporting purpose with passion and dedication."

Mineral Name: Copper

Archangel: Raphael

Color: Orange metallic ore

Healing Properties: Copper eases joint pain exceptionally well. It also increases self-esteem and self-awareness and helps establish emotional boundaries.

Message: "Flexibility is required when participating in this life journey, as there are myriad experiences of a magnificent nature to absorb while in your human shape. You agreed to have emotions and live contained in this earthly form, all the while knowing that energy is your perfect state. I commend your bravery. I've encouraged your race in their progress by acting as a survival tool and an instrument of healing for those in crippling physical pain, and my blessings encourage you to continue stretching your mind and body. Learn to respect and support your health by setting appropriate boundaries on all levels, including the physical and emotional. Rejoice in this incarnation, and seek out new challenges such as those found in yoga and dance—coordinating all your aspects will provide a foundation of youthful movement evermore. I trust you'll continue to light the world with the benefits of my properties."

Mineral Name: Coral

Archangel:
Ariel

Colors: Pink, red,
and white

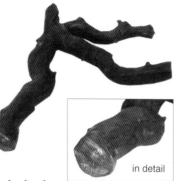

in detail

Healing Properties:
Coral is a precious gift
from the sea that supports the heal-
ing of bone structures and eases emotional distress.

Message: "Found in current and former ocean floors,
I bring synchronistic gifts of stimulating health. From
jewelry to supplements, my skeletal form fortifies the
human body in plentiful variations. I hold memories of
the sea in my being, helping you navigate the transforma-
tional emotional waters in which you swim. I ground you
in the blissful love of Mother Earth and Father Sky, clos-
ing any chasms of separation. Know that your foundation
is strong, and nurture all aspects of your health by feeding your body and soul appropriately. In doing so, you
derive the blessings of effectiveness that support your
light mission and, ultimately, the successful completion
of this cycle."

Mineral Name:
Danburite

Pronunciation:
"DAN-bur-ite"

Archangel: Raziel

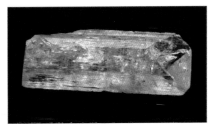

Colors: Clear, pink, white, and yellow

Healing Properties: This shaman's stone has clear, pure, and intense energy that unlocks barriers and blockages with joy. It's a powerful healing tool that's best used in conjunction with other crystals.

Message: "As a high-frequency corridor to the state of enlightenment, I am a companion to shamans, wizards, and priestesses. I don't tolerate confusion or fear and will quickly bring them to the surface, so you can expect faith and trust in my presence. I promise to guide you in astral travels to adventures that transcend your current sensibilities and establish new thinking. I open your eyes to the possibilities of instant manifestation, vibrational healing, and telepathic communication on all levels . . . and more. Recognize that I'm a healer versed in identifying the location and cause of disease, and that I work best in conjunction with skilled practitioners. Call on me now without delay, and allow my crystal friends to induce additional healing momentum."

Mineral Name: Desert Rose

Archangels: Azrael, Jeremiel, and Raguel

Colors: Brown, tan, white, and pale yellow

Healing Properties: The desert rose enhances feelings of well-being, and an understanding of your unique, personal value in the universal plan.

Message: "A delicate bud birthed from sand, I'm here to spread happiness through beauty, and to remind you to embrace the blossoming of self. Each soul is as unique as a snowflake, perfect in its composition and a loving gift from the Creator. Still, the greatest pleasure is found in unity, so come together in groups to relax and confide in one another while experiencing the cooperative spirit of love in reflection. As you accept individuality without comparison, you become a mirror for love, and the world continues developing a deeper sense of community and interdependence."

Mineral Name: Diamond

Archangel: Raziel

Colors: Blue, clear (white), pink, yellow

Healing Properties: A diamond reflects all colors of the rainbow and chakra system. It's a stone of clarity, commitment, and communication that enhances prosperity, love, and spirituality while also focusing on personal purpose.

Message: "I display the full spectrum of hues in my role as a bridge of light into the chakras, where I amplify each energy exchange. As incarnated nobility of the mineral kingdom, my brilliance is renowned as a reflection of purity, abundance, and devotion, and I soar with force toward Heaven's call. Engaging with my energy demands unity, genuine motivation, unconditional acceptance, and vigorous dedication.

"As a symbol of partnership, I'm best suited for shared experiences that take human spirits to a place of profound love. I channel Divine energy and angelic grace to welcome those who are willing to step into commitment with an open heart, prepared to learn and grow with one another. Will you journey with me?"

Mineral Name: Dioptase

Pronunciation:
"Di-OP-taze"

Archangel: Raphael

Color: Deep emerald green

Healing Properties: This stone aids in creating life balance. It's a powerful healing crystal that's used to create harmony while you work toward achieving your personal goals.

Message: "As a master stone for healers, uniting with those of you dedicated to the betterment of health on all levels allows me to open new channels of vibrational medicine. Many of you are familiar with me through work you did in past lives; today, I'm reintroducing techniques from past civilizations through crystal therapy. Our renewed partnership leads to original discoveries in healing, with a primary focus on clearing old wounds, and I teach you to alleviate buried pain by learning how to play again. It's time to think as a child and act with abandon, feeling complete expectation of good in every action and thought."

Mineral Name: Emerald

Archangels:
Haniel, Jophiel, Raziel,
and Raphael

Color: Green

Healing Properties: Emerald is a stone of the heart that's outstanding for dream work and meditation, as it deepens spirituality and consciousness. It's also an all-purpose healing stone.

Message: "With regal stature, I accept the honors bestowed upon me by Heaven's hand, and I guard your heart's essence, which is Divine love. Co-creating with me requires your full attention and lucidity since I operate at God's speed, and from thoughts to manifestation, our energies join to deliver the highest good. Behold—the mantle of universal graciousness is draped upon your life as I compel you to function at the highest levels, ensuring that you walk an illuminated path with the brilliance of love as your guide. All you require and desire is yours when you focus on service, for if you respond with generosity, so shall you receive goodness in all matters. Similarly, when I'm in the hands of a healer, I expand their accessible knowledge and provide the strongest of green rays to heal broken hearts."

Mineral Name: Fluorite

Pronunciation:
"FLOOR-ite"

Archangels: Chamuel,
Raphael, Raziel, and Uriel

Colors: Blue, clear, green, purple, and yellow

Healing Properties: This mineral does a wonderful job
of accessing your deeper awareness and promoting
spiritual growth. It's a powerful healing stone that helps
ground your energy and improve your focus.

Message: "Standing in unity, we present ourselves to
assist in your process of authentication. We carry gentle
combinations of potent healing abilities that trigger meditative states, peeling back layers of personality and preparing you for vision quests to meet your authentic self. We're
frequently called upon during contemplation to initiate
meetings with ascended masters and guides. Yet, we also
provide clear thinking to keep day-to-day activities
focused and moving smoothly, and we serve as personal
trainers in healing to individuals interested in the art and
practice of crystal therapy."

Mineral Name: Garnet

Pronunciation: "GAR-net"

Archangels: Gabriel, Haniel, and Raphael

Colors: Red, yellow, green, brown, pink, and black

Healing Properties: Garnet stimulates passion, creativity, and intention, as well as working to heal blood-related diseases.

Message: "Are you feeling uncertain about what you're here to accomplish? Is there a clog in your creativity, or do you want a richer sense of passion in your life? Yes, I thought so—that's why you brought me home. With color as bold as blood, I activate and help shift energy, which frees you to experiment in new ways. I remove fear, tempering your concerns by reminding you that your thoughts create experiences. When you keep focused with an attitude of gratitude, the world replaces woes with *Whoas!* of astonishment and happiness as you realize and manifest what were once merely dreams."

Mineral Name:
Gold

Archangels:
Michael, Raphael,
and Uriel

Color: Metallic yellow ore

Healing Properties: Gold is an all-purpose healer that stabilizes, purifies, and balances while presenting the male energy of action to the world. It speaks of abundance and well-being.

Message: "As a conveyer of the Christ light, I am one of the most precious elements. In my metallic form, I serve as a partner to many in the mineral kingdom, elevating their vibrations to the highest platform. I'm reminiscent of the sun, brilliant and life sustaining, with prosperity and wealth reflected in my luster. As straightforward as male energy, I exude an air of competence and fulfillment, adding a sense of confidence to those who wear me, and a sense of stability to those who barter with me. My true currency is a pure form of energy exchange."

Mineral Name: Hematite

Pronunciation:
"HEE-muh-tite"

Archangels:
Jophiel and Michael

Color: Shiny gray

Healing Properties: This stone enhances personal magnetism, optimism, will, and courage. In addition, it strengthens physical and etheric bodies and acts as a grounding tool.

Message: "Embodied in my weighty form is a direct link to feelings of stability and security, and it's my honor to escort you as you explore new levels of self-understanding. By mirroring the beauty and burdens of each individual, I become a catalyst of choice so that you and I can expose any layers of negative residue you may have. We prepare them for clearing and introduce happiness by increasing optimism, risk taking, and willpower. As you shift your perspective, relinquishing control and increasing your trust will build up your personal magnetism. In addition, the release process can improve your sleep patterns, relieve health concerns, and have a calming effect on your personal and business environments."

Mineral Name: Jade

Archangels: Raphael and Raziel

Colors: Green, lavender, white, black, yellow, red, brown, and blue, with creamy (*nephrite*) or translucent (*jadeite*) characteristics

Healing Properties: This prosperity stone improves health and assists with past-life recall and ancient wisdom, especially within Asian traditions.

Message: "I offer the gifts of serenity, tranquility, wisdom, prosperity, and a feeling of soothing calmness. You may wear me close to your skin as a reminder of the blessings from Spirit. I act as a conduit for transition from this plane to the next, creating a space of loving peace, so hold me in your hand or rest me against your forehead to initiate conversations with those who have gone before. Place me with those entering the corridors of new beginnings in order to ease the feeling of separation. I've been the adornment of royalty and a weapon of war, yet always my purpose is to heal, stimulating inspiration and growth while reminding you all of the abundant and loving Universe."

Mineral Name: Jasper

Archangels: Ariel and Metatron

Colors: Red, brown, yellow, pink, green, blue, and purple

Healing Properties: Jasper's color family works with the chakras to balance, recalibrate, and heal. Its soft energy also bolsters organizational skills and quickens project completion.

Message: "As a nurturer with gentle, nudging guidance that's as familiar as parental love, I offer respite from the chaos of daily events. I facilitate clear thinking, organization, and completion of projects by working with you to focus through your open energy centers. Combinations of my colors align naturally for chakra meditations and clearing."

Jasper Variations

<u>Ocean Jasper</u>

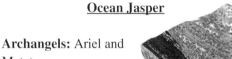

Archangels: Ariel and Metatron

Colors: Pink, green, and white

Healing Properties: Ocean jasper embodies the heart-healing properties of the colors pink and green. In addition, its round markings stimulate complete breaths and movement of energy.

Message: "Circular movements abound within my pattern of pink, green, and white. Just as the waves of the ocean move in harmonic rhythm, I remind you to breathe in a continuous motion to clear the debris of toxins within your body."

<u>Picture Jasper</u>

Archangel: Ariel

Colors: Variations of earth tones such as brown, green, and red, which look as though Mother Earth used a paintbrush to create a beautiful scene.

Healing Properties: This is the perfect companion for bringing nature's healing indoors. It also reminds you to embrace a regular meditation practice.

Message: "Nature paints her portraits within my frame, so stop to see the majestic view of the Earth captured in me. I kindle stronger relationships with Mother Earth as you invite me inside to be a companion in your daily work."

Mineral Name: Kunzite

Pronunciation:
"KUN-site"

Archangels:
Jophiel and Raguel

Colors: Pink, lavender, clear, yellow, and green

Healing Properties: Kunzite opens your heart to love and helps create balanced partnerships. In this way, it promotes peace on Earth, reducing individual separation and stress.

Message: "The heightened power of feminine vibration is my salutation. I lend you my strength to remove your layers of pain from this and other times, which will create within you the freedom of unconditional love. The decision to be whole begins with you, for no one else has the power to heal your life. Step forward to examine and release the cause of your disconnection, and then reclaim your truest essence: joy. Burdens of the heart dissipate through acknowledgment, acceptance, and forgiveness, so renew your innocence in the precious moments that you expose the barrier of self-imposed separation and reestablish self-trust."

Mineral Name: Kyanite

Pronunciation: "KI-uh-nite"

Archangels: Gabriel,
Metatron, and Raguel

Color: Pearlescent blue with white

Healing Properties: Kyanite connects you with youthful zest and optimism. It also encourages you to speak from the heart with trust and experience the joy of life.

Message: "I provide a sense of gentle love with the strength to speak your personal truth. I help you step out of the way and allow information to flow by eliminating blockages in the throat chakra and removing your fears. By opening the door to the exploration of higher understanding and cosmic consciousness, I provide new perspectives of channeled clarity that inspire pioneering solutions in areas of discord on this plane. My gift is the ability to discern truth when we act as partners in self-realization and self-actualization, so work with me in these experiences. Ask yourself: Is this the present or the past resurfacing? Call upon me to resolve conflict, both within the self and with others."

Mineral Name: Labradorite

Pronunciation:
"LAB-ruh-dore-ite"

Archangels: Haniel,
Michael, and Raziel

Color: Dark gray with iridescent shades of green, blue, and yellow

Healing Properties: Representing the temple of stars, labradorite assists in discovering your destiny and provides clarity of inner sight.

Message: "Descended from galaxies and reflecting wizardry within, I'm the stone of internal connection. I link communication from the solar plexus to the brow, engaging you in new levels of contact with the Divine. Work with me with your eyes closed, as your body relaxes into its natural state. My energy allows safe access to wisdom, so you can travel to new dimensions; and my strength is bold, so be prepared to move quickly with increasing rhythms. Summon me when you're ready to journey beyond the confines of what's known, and when you're prepared to expand your consciousness."

Mineral Name: Lapis Lazuli

Pronunciation:
"LAP-is LA-zuh-lee"

Archangels: Michael,
Raziel, and Zadkiel

Colors: Royal to dark blue with interspersed flecks of gold and white

Healing Properties: This stone expands your senses by opening your third eye, and connects your heart and head to create balance and interdependence in your relationships.

Message: "Clan member, I call on you to rise and speak the truth. Can you hear the echoing voices of the past? Ask for guidance, and you'll be given wisdom. Accept your mission, speak out, and remove fear, replacing it with knowledge as your voice is lifted unto Heaven. I share with you the royal legacy of the kings and queens who favored my brilliant blue as a sign of power, for your words are mighty. Use me to teach by word and deed; serve as healer to those who haven't found their voice, and bless those who have. Know that you are protected, and go forth."

Mineral Name: Larimar

Pronunciation:
"LAR-uh-mar"

Archangels: Ariel and Raguel

Color: Soft aqua blue with white intermixed, reminiscent of tropical island waters and cresting whitecap waves

Healing Properties: Larimar's gentle, innocent energy recalls that of the unicorn, and it aids in releasing depression with its calming spirit.

Message: "I'm enchanting, inspiring sweet remembrances of dolphins spinning with water sprites in the ocean waves, jubilant fairies flitting between flowers, and unicorns lingering undisturbed in fields of grass. Look unto me for a private vision of the self you hold within, for mirrored in my face is truth, the purity of spirit realized. With me, your heart is unsullied by fear and loss of innocence, and instead you feel glorious wholeness. Choose to access Divine wisdom, peace, and tranquility as I bridge the realms of consciousness to bring you equilibrium in your current form. I can show you castle views from the clouds that recall serenity to your once-broken heart and wrap it in the blessings of love."

Mineral Name:
Lemurian Quartz

Pronunciation:
"Le-MUR-ee-an"

Archangels: Haniel and Raziel

Color: Clear quartz with a soft pink tinge and notable ridges on the sides

Healing Properties: This rare, powerful stone helps connect you with ancient information from past civilizations, and it's an excellent telepathic and healing partner. In addition, it promotes self-confidence through strengthening your focus and concentration.

Message: "I'm the remaining record of the civilization known as Lemuria, which was once a continent crossing the earth and now exists in other dimensions. The keys of understanding from this time are found within my structure. Those called to me know the power of vibration, color, and sound . . . and they communicate without words, understanding the intangible ability to link with love. Healers, too, are drawn to me, for I keep the sacred secrets of temple rooms. As the rainbow captured in crystal form, I assist you in evolving, yet you must be pure of heart to activate me, for I know destruction and won't be a party to it again. My mysteries will stay guarded until I know you and establish trust. Don't search me out, but be patient, for I'll arrive at the appropriate time, and you'll recognize my familiar energy once again."

Mineral Name:
Lepidolite

Pronunciation:
"Lih-PIH-duh-lite"

Archangels:
Raguel and Raphael

Colors: Lavender to pink, with specks of sparkling mica

Healing Properties: This relaxing stone soothes and heals stress while strengthening your discovery of your Higher Self.

Message: "Breathe. You so often forget the importance of your breath, which is the life force that energizes, stabilizes, and centers you. Hold me in your hands and feel waves of calm wash over your being as they bring rejuvenation, which is my word and reminder to you. When the whirlwind of activities overflows in your life, call on me to show you the hues of tranquil sunsets merging on the horizon as the day is completed and night prepares to quiet your soul. Release the burdens you carry and allow your emotions to ease. I support your clear sight, guiding you into dreamtime and helping you remember what is written in the Room of Records. Relax and ask, Dear One."

Mineral Name:
Malachite

Pronunciation:
"MAL-uh-kite"

Archangel: Raphael

Color: Rich, deep green with ribbons of lighter shades and patterns reminiscent of the third eye

Healing Properties: This strong healing stone builds physical health by strengthening your heart. It also attracts abundance by working from the heart's life purpose.

Message: "Recall the sustenance and source of love with me. I serve as a key to heart awareness, ready to assist you in the journey of discovering and experiencing oneness in all ways. Complete and perfect in individual forms, no two of my stones are alike, and in that uniqueness you'll find the beauty of acceptance. Learn here to accentuate that which makes you distinctive, along with the grace of knowing that you're also part of the one life essence, for although we all appear different at first glance, the commonalities of our hearts are evident. I'm here to help magnify this power of love in your life, so invite me to join you in meditation so that I may amplify your intention to heal on all levels and across all directions of time and movement, opening you to receive the gifts of universal support and love."

Mineral Name: Moldavite

Pronunciation:
"MOLE-duh-vite"

Archangels:
Ariel, Raphael, and Raziel

Color: Green

Healing Properties: Moldavite has an extraordinary vibration that elevates consciousness with awareness and helps connect you with ascended masters.

Message: "Are you ready to fly with me upon the echoing vibrations of my original descent? As a meteorite, I was fiercely burning fire in the sky until I crashed into the open arms of Mother Earth. I've stayed hidden until just recently, when the invitation for initiation was issued. Many now have heard the call sent by the dolphins and whales, and it's in their language of wisdom that I'm activated as a healing modality. I'm a great power and demand respect, and when it's given, I can be of tremendous assistance to those prepared in body, mind, and spirit for the journey of discovery. Caution is warranted for the uninitiated, however, since I can also be overwhelming for the ill-prepared. Exercise care, and connect with me only in moderation."

Mineral Name: Moonstone

Archangel: Haniel

Colors: Creamy white, blue, pink, and yellow

Healing Properties: This stone of new beginnings is a talisman of good fortune that assists in positive change and protects those who are traveling.

Message: "I'm a talisman for women with my ever-present moon energy that surrounds my friends, enhancing their femininity and beauty. I captivate those who gaze at me, inducing a quiet feeling of sensuality and a calling to soul-mate partnership. Male/female balance is essential, for when you live in coordination of yin and yang principles, the universal flow moves without interruption, allowing consistent support and attracting experiences and people that encourage your purpose and focus. Although I'm an influence with feminine power (nurturer, creator, and lover), all humans can feel and share in these roles; thus, my vibration is a tribute to the breadth of your possibilities."

Mineral Name:
Obsidian

Pronunciation:
"Ob-SIH-dee-uhn"

Archangels:
Jophiel, Michael,
and Raziel

Colors: Black, rainbow, green, mahogany, smoky, golden sheen, and snowflake

Healing Properties: Obsidian is nature's gift of protection for sensitive individuals. It dispels negativity and pain and repels unwelcome feelings.

Message: "As a wizard stone, I'm a guardian to those who know me. Don't fear any negativity, for a protective shield wraps around you when I'm called into service. Invite me to walk with you, especially when traveling or when in crowds, in order to dispel energy that's out of alignment or without integrity. It's my honor to join you in peaceful journey."

Obsidian Variations

Rainbow Obsidian

Archangel: Raziel

Color: Translucent black with hints of circular luminosity, usually with shades of gray, green, and blue

Healing Properties: This mineral promotes understanding of the present in relation to the past and helps you release old beliefs and judgments.

Message: "Join with me in celebration as the colors of the rainbow glisten from my center. In contemplation, gaze into my face and feel elation flow through you, reigniting the innocent wonders found in your childhood eyes and reclaiming the memory of joy."

<u>Snowflake Obsidian</u>

Archangels: Raguel and Uriel

Color: Black with flecks of white "snowflakes"

Healing Properties: Snowflake obsidian reduces fear and rebalances your focus, which enables positive thinking.

Message: "I encapsulate the balance of light and dark through my stark contrasts of black and white. When stress and fear fill you, heed my healing counsel to release those thoughts that don't support you and replace them with angelic guidance and love."

❋

Mineral Name: Onyx

Pronunciation: "AH-nix"

Archangels: Haniel, Raguel, and Raziel

Colors: Black, blue, green, and yellow

Healing Properties: Onyx increases your awareness of visions and dreams. It emphasizes self-control and grounding, so it's good for individuals who would like to increase their concentration.

Message: "Dream with me under your pillow, and you'll recall the lessons of nighttime and begin to immediately and peacefully incorporate them into your life. I join you as a stabilizing force in order to add a dimension of self-trust when you're struggling to find your sense of balance in the precarious events of living. In learning to trust, you're introduced to a world of peace, and your willingness to accept vulnerability establishes a broadening sense of community. With me, you can solidify the increasing focus and concentration that emerge with your self-acceptance. Let go and relax, for I will guide you."

Mineral Name: Opal

Archangels: Haniel, Metatron, and Uriel

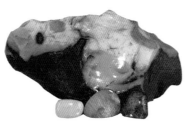

Colors: An iridescent display of rainbow colors: often white, orange, black, blue, pink, and purple; they can be either clear or milky

Healing Properties: Harmony is the essence of this stone, which derives from its gift in balancing all levels of your being.

Message: "As ever changing as sand shifting on the beach, I'm light reflecting light. I offer you harmony, radiance in all your aspects, and light in darkness (just as the day cycles from sunlight to moonlight) in order to create the perfect alignment of thought and action. Will you accept this gift? Emotions intensify with me, for I see your passion and enhance the releasement of lingering patterns. My activation dissipates karmic ties and produces the desire to let go of old wounds. As you claim the Divine power within, so shall your life reflect light and embrace the tender strength of true love. Begin with self-acceptance and patience in order to harmonize the embodiment of male and female within all."

Mineral Name:
Pearl

Archangel: Haniel

Colors: Luminous
white and gray-black

Healing Properties: The pearl is a symbol of integrity, purity, and grace. It acts as a special conduit to the heavens and works especially well with colored stones.

Message: "Although at first I'm an irritant within the very core of a being, I emerge as a pristine image of beauty and transcendence. Isn't it so in your life? Once the cause of grave pain, a problem can give birth to new perspective or a more refined self if you know that you can choose to reach acceptance and compassion by choice. How do you choose to live: with intensity, commitment, and love? If so, then wear me as a symbol of self-awareness, for I'm an infusion of Divine connection through water, and I symbolize emotional growth and readiness."

Mineral Name: Peridot

Pronunciation:
"PAIR-uh-doh"

Archangel: Raguel

Colors: Translucent olive
and yellowish to dark green

Healing Properties: Peridot clears the way for your heart to feel. It also assists in creating prosperity in all areas of life and is excellent for understanding relationships with honesty and integrity.

Message: "Nestled in volcanic remnants in the Earth's crust, I'm found unexpectedly along the beach. I'm quieter now than in times past, since the world's focus differs from the days of Camelot. Today, I stand as a guardian of hope, wisdom, generosity, abundance, and compassion. You may find me most often polished and worn in jewelry as a gentle reminder of your own gifts. Embrace me, and invite me into your home in my natural state. I share Divine miracles and beauty with you by intensifying your manifestation abilities and acting as a guide in realizing that which you hold closest to your heart. Blessings unto you, Dear Ones, as you journey forward."

Mineral Name:
Platinum

Archangels:
Metatron and Raziel

Color: Metallic silver gray

Healing Properties: This high-level conductor moves energy with exceptional speed and is outstanding in combination with diamonds.

Message: "I access the fastest vibrational corridor generated by the metal ores. My ferocious speed and intense, pulsating energy exhilarate those equipped to accept them. When used with stones in jewelry, I weave a magnetic grid that deepens the overall combination, which constructs a new road to meditative consciousness and your intuitive abilities. Not surprisingly, there's a renewed interest in me at the moment, so there will be many who now heed the call to become lightworkers as I expand Heaven's bridge to Earth."

Mineral Name: Pyrite

Pronunciation:
"PIE-rite"

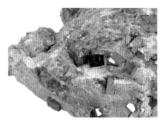

Archangel: Uriel

Color: Yellowish-gold cubes, often called fool's gold

Healing Properties: This mineral assists you in creating material abundance, and meditation with pyrite increases your ability to balance energies by providing a stabilizing force.

Message: "Your brethren knew me from the start, when I gave the spark of fire to humankind and the gift of reflection as a mirror. I ground you with awareness and protection; I clarify your focus and illustrate abundance. My shape is the Divine cubic design of manifestation. What is it that you desire? Clarity, action, and trust will bring it into your life. Shrouded in my protection, you're free to move between the seen and unseen, accessing the reality that is truth. God supports your quest and supplies all your needs, for the Universe is abundant in every way."

Mineral Name: Quartz

Archangels: Ariel, Gabriel, Haniel, Michael, Raphael, Raziel, and Sandalphon

Colors: Clear, blue, green, rose, smoky (brown), and tangerine

Healing Properties: This crystal draws blessings of all kinds into your life. It's believed to bring the stars into the soul, enhance spiritual awareness, and intensify your awakening process. It also works to harmonize energies.

Message: "Alpha and omega in the mineral kingdom, I reign without question. From my foundation, the spark of possibilities is sent to begin facilitating your deeper attunement with the unseen. My vibrational pattern serves as a launch point, providing tangible evidence that energy transformation functions as an amplifier, generator, receiver, and cleanser. When in doubt, select me to act as the custodian of your intent so that you may experience the gifts of Divine guidance, motivation, and clarity."

Quartz Variations

Blue Quartz

Archangels: Gabriel and Sandalphon

Healing Properties: This helpful tool for discussing emotional issues is also an effective purification agent when cleansing your environment. In addition, it supports harmonious interactions and communication.

Message: "I walk with you in patience, ready to assist in cleansing so that you may speak your truth without hesitation. Service with love is my message: Reach beyond yourself through words and actions to unleash your talents and skills to their highest potential and greatest good."

Green Quartz

Archangel: Gabriel

Healing Properties: Green quartz inspires creativity, attracts success and abundance, and promotes an intuitive capability coupled with love.

Message: "Add me to your environment when you'd like to increase abundance, creativity, and perception.

The manifestation of all you dream is already complete. Intention and thoughts accelerate your acceptance or denial, so watch them carefully in designing your life, and I will support you in this."

Rose Quartz

Archangel: Ariel

Color: Pink

Healing Properties: This rosy stone facilitates heart-healing openness to love on all levels and focuses your energy on self-love. It also fosters inner peace, tranquility, and healing.

Message: "I embody the essence of authentic love. By opening your heart chakra to encourage complete self-acceptance, I help soothe wounds of sadness and distrust with enveloping feelings of unconditional love that allow forgiveness to occur. I remind you that all feel joy and sorrow when they're in human form, and that emotions are a gift. Operating with me promotes both this regard for yourself and inclusive tolerance.

"Wear me with grace, for I can help attract romantic partners through my soft color's welcoming glow and my calm receptivity, tempered with the strength of feminine power."

Smoky Quartz

Archangel: Michael

Colors: Light brown or light gray (translucent)

Healing Properties: This superb meditation crystal grounds and centers you, helps eliminate your fears, and enhances awareness of your dreams.

Message: "Stabilization during meditation is key, and I assist you in maintaining that grounded perspective while raising your energetic field. Acting as an anchor, I provide a fresh method of releasing fear by accepting and reprogramming your beliefs into champion-level goals. I'm an excellent stone for balancing male energy and optimizing your potential on this earthly plane."

Tangerine Quartz

Archangel: Gabriel

Color: Light orange

Healing Properties: Tangerine quartz balances your emotions, calming and soothing you while increasing your artistry and receptivity to Divine inspiration.

Message: "Creativity flows through me, stirring and supporting your driving desire to shape the dreams long held within your heart. Place me with honor in an area reflective of expression, for whether I'm in the office, garden, studio, or kitchen, I'll assist you in translating your vision into reality."

Mineral Name: Rhodocrosite

Pronunciation:
"Roh-duh-KROH-site"

Archangels: Jeremiel,
Metatron, and Michael

Colors: Creamy pink and white

Healing Properties: Rhodocrosite eases moments of change by serving as a bridge between your upper and lower chakras, which creates a balanced, loving approach to life.

Message: "The human experience is a blessed one, sometimes exhilarating and sometimes challenging. It's laden with karmic relationships, individual and societal expectations, and complex emotions; yet there's also great love, joy, and passion surrounding you. As you begin to find the quiet center within yourself, I come forward and activate your heart chakra, connecting your lower and upper energy centers. With concentration and intent, I facilitate change by establishing a bond of love that engulfs your being and relieves fear. I remind you to approach life in accordance with your beliefs, and that committing to yourself means acting with integrity in all areas of your life."

Mineral Name: Rhodonite

Pronunciation:
"ROH-duh-nite"

Archangels:
Metatron and Sandalphon

Colors: Creamy rose and black

Healing Properties: Use this crystal in toning practices to escalate sound and amplify connection. It's also an excellent heart stone that helps shed old patterns and pain.

Message: "I am sound sensitive, which makes me an excellent partner in sound healing or in a toning practice. One aspect of my role is assistance in the sound chamber re-creation on the earthly plane. The sound chamber is the temple (which now exists in the astral plane) that uses sound, in combination with color and crystals, to accelerate vibrational frequencies. I can help you anchor this increased vibration on Earth and in your physical body to help you awaken your soul's healing memories. Try linking my vibrational sequences with chanting to further magnify your output of intention and receptivity to information. As I accompany you on this journey, I ask you to review situations and relationships with a new eye in order to really see what isn't working and recognize your outdated beliefs, patterns, and reactions. It's time for you to actualize as you were intended to do, so listen to the guidance of your heart and walk forward in peace."

Mineral Name: Ruby

Archangels:
Jophiel and Michael

Colors: Pink to deep blood red

Healing Properties: This gem strengthens love, induces awareness of your heart's connections, and allows you to care for yourself so that you may receive devotion.

Message: "I call to those willing to walk in the fire of action and self-awareness: Rise up and come unto me, for the lifeblood of creativity and breath of purposeful movement pulsate within both of us. Act with intention and watch the world open as you share your light. I'm energy personified, one of the royal clan who lay upon the ancient breastplate of activation. Ask me to show you the direction of your agreement, then sit with me in reflection to feel the knowing clarity of purpose wash over you. Join me in embracing the power of potential realized. We exist in a continuum, never alone, so reach for me as you prepare yourself and invite truth to reign."

Mineral Name: Sapphire

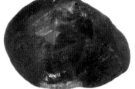

Archangels:
Michael and Raziel

Colors: Translucent blue, yellow, green, black, and purple

Healing Properties: Sapphire clears mind chatter, assists with organizational skills, and enhances your intuitive abilities.

Message: "As a star of the skies brought to Earth, I blend with you to initiate the awakening of all your intuitive senses. Trust me, for together we quiet your mind so that truth is heard. Wear me when moments of uncertainty seem to prevail, so you may feel calmness and serenity instead. It's within that seekers find the road of purpose, and when the heart speaks, the void of questioning is lit, illuminating the brilliance contained in each being. With clarity and consciousness, your soul rises to fulfill your responsibility of humanness with joy."

Mineral Name:
Selenite

Pronunciation:
"SEH-luh-nite"

Archangels: Haniel and Michael

Colors: Clear, orange, red, brown, and green blue

Healing Properties: Selenite enables access to information from the Pleiades. It also helps heal negativity and fears, and provides alignment and cleansing abilities.

Message: "Friend of the Moon Goddess, I'm comprised of layers of knowledge from the cosmos. Traveling from afar to be with you in these days of shifting awareness, I hold the instinctive acumen of star people. The feel of my weight within your hand is as familiar as the sword that once defended Heaven's gate as Michael stood guard, and with me there is always safety, comfort, and peace. In blended cadence, we can cleanse the environment and individual bodies of negative energy residue. When you're out of alignment, simply focus and envision that the hooks, cords, and threads of severed connections now exist in harmony and are refilled with love."

Mineral Name: Silver

Archangel: Haniel

Color: Metallic gray

Healing Properties:
Silver's feminine, receptive energy softly engages with stones to escalate their properties.

Message: "As luminous as the moon, and reflecting the face of the feminine Divine, I hold the unbridled strength of her wisdom within me. When I contact another in the mineral clan, I activate that aspect of their being to its greatest potential. It's my mission to allay the misconception that feminine power is less than male power—rather, it's different and must be honored as such in each of us. Learning to harness these differences will bring a greater continuity to the world and a return to peaceful coexistence."

Mineral Name: Sodalite

Pronunciation: "SOH-duh-lite"

Archangels: Gabriel, Jeremiel, Raphael, and Zadkiel

Color: Dark blue with white veins

Healing Properties: This stone supports you in letting go of control issues. It's also an excellent third-eye stone that increases your psychic awareness.

Message: "I understand addictions and the course they can cause a life to take. Only an honest review and candor with yourself and others can break the cycle, for communication is the cornerstone of transformation. Your ability to be of service to others, and to lift your light to help them, will improve as you move forward. I'm here to support you in that process of opening up and becoming vulnerable. Ease your fear by finding written or spoken words to guide you in your journey, and practice with me by your side. Patterns are broken with steady patience and self-love, so release control and accept support from those around you in all dimensions. You're safe, and the blocks you once placed for your protection are removed so that all your senses are rejuvenated."

Mineral Name: Sugilite

Pronunciation:
"SOO-gil-ite"

Archangel: Michael

Color: Purple with a hint of black

Healing Properties: Sugilite amplifies your pineal and pituitary gland activity in order to encourage the connection of physical and spiritual bodies.

Message: "As a channel activator, I route communication to and through beings, so if you agree to participate in the process of Divine interaction, you'll connect with distinguished masters. No one can force you to accept the opportunity to extend beyond yourself, since acting as a vehicle of voice for other realms is only done by choice. If you're in agreement, working with me opens areas once impeded as the *clairs* [intuitive senses] intensify, and you experience richer communication. Most often, I work with those already serving in their mission of light, supporting their efforts by calibrating all aspects of their bodies for optimal output."

Mineral Name:
Tiger's-Eye

Archangels:
Michael and Uriel

Colors: Gold and red

Healing Properties: This stone enhances your connection with your personal power and strengthens your resolve. In addition, it improves your insights, softens stubbornness, and fosters self-confidence.

Message: "As golden rays captured in physical form, I bring to light the possibilities offered by confidence and trust in the Universe. You walk along the path of purpose in full majesty when I'm by your side; in me, you find the delights of accomplishment through your strength of conviction, steady focus, and clear vision. I'm accentuated male energy to those who crave the ability to stand firm in their beliefs and to show the world their truth while sharing their unique gifts. In my golden form, I work directly with the sacral and solar-plexus chakras by adding potency and stability and increasing poise and self-esteem."

Tiger's-Eye Variation

Red Tiger's-Eye

Archangel: Gabriel

Healing Properties: This variety of tiger's-eye builds your confidence by accessing your inner wisdom and guidance, which makes it the perfect stone for public speaking.

Message: "I'm an excellent friend to the facilitator, teacher, and speaker since I engage all channels of communication and combine your inner wisdom with learned expertise in complete confidence. I establish an easy exchange of ideas and exploration of beliefs while encouraging astute understanding with empathetic awareness, especially when working with groups."

❊

Mineral Name: Topaz

Archangels: Chamuel, Gabriel, Jophiel, Michael, Raziel

Colors: Blue, pink, golden, and clear (white)

Healing Properties: This master stone vibrates at a heightened level that brings information and healing at an accelerated rate for those with open hearts.

Message: "In blissful unification, my clan steps forward to share our story. We've traveled through the annals of history as precious gifts between lovers, royal adornments, talismans, and healing tools, and our time is here once again. We welcome the opportunity to perform in partnership with you, escalating the planetary vibration through our personal interactions."

Topaz Variations

Blue Topaz

Archangel: Gabriel

Healing Properties:
As a writers' stone, blue topaz helps you communicate from your heart since it aligns your creativity and purpose.

Message: "Writers know my cool eloquence, as I bring them gifts of streaming words—just as rivers flow into the ocean. A single spring of reflection becomes a tide of ideas that generates new understandings and cultivates philosophical conversations."

Golden Topaz

Archangel: Michael

Healing Properties: This joyful gem partners with you to attract wealth, well-being, and love, in addition to helping you fully open your crown chakra to heavenly exchange.

Message: "As a champion of confidence, I activate your solar plexus so that you radiate personal power with integrity and honor. Happily, I assist you in creating abundance in all ways. Wear me when you need an energetic lift, and renewed excitement about life and hope are yours."

Pink Topaz

Archangels: Chamuel and Jophiel

Healing Properties: This aphrodisiac attracts love on many levels, and as a heart-chakra stone, it amplifies your ability to care for others unconditionally.

Message: "The passionate nature of love corresponds to the beauty of my color, which is a rare gift to be cherished. I am a confidant to those wholeheartedly ready to encounter and embrace their soul partner."

White Topaz

Archangel: Raziel

Healing Properties: White topaz heightens your vibrational levels, clears old energy, and increases your feelings of connection with the Divine.

Message: "Bond with me to purge stuck energies, including those from other lifetimes, and we'll eliminate those outdated patterns with focused intention. Request assistance from the Divine to rid yourself of the unfortunate continuation of old beliefs, and you may hear the celestial chorus of celebration."

Mineral Name: Tourmaline

Pronunciation: "TOUR-muh-leen"

Archangels: Azrael, Chamuel, Gabriel, Metatron, Michael, and Raphael

Colors: Black, green, pink, watermelon, red, yellow, and blue

Healing Properties: This significant clan of healing stones commands energy on its own. When used with other stones, tourmaline creates a chakra bridge of spiritual expansion.

Message: "As a family of healers, uniquely potent and exceptional in combination, we're providing an array of services in support of evolution and ascension. Hold us close to your skin, for our vibration in rings and pendants adds beauty and strength to your mission of light. We work gladly with those who embrace the beings of stars that bring new medicine into this world. Individually powerful, each of our colors transcends barriers of belief and understanding to culminate in facilitating shifts of consciousness. When we're used in chakra combinations, profound alterations occur that escalate the dynamic forces of unity and healing change."

Tourmaline Variations

<u>Black Tourmaline</u>

Archangels: Gabriel and Michael

Healing Properties: This stone is excellent for dispelling negativity in all forms, especially the electromagnetic vibrations associated with cell phones and computers. It also stimulates practicality with creativity in order to help you achieve your desired goals.

Message: "A shield of magnetic protection envelops you when I'm near, so invite me into your business settings to guide and look after you, and place me near your computer to reduce stress."

Green Tourmaline

Archangels: Azrael and Raphael

Healing Properties: As a rejuvenating stone, green tourmaline unblocks your heart chakra so that you can experience the joy and zest of life.

Message: "I'm a heart opener and an oasis of refreshment for your soul. Drink in my flow of fortification and healing properties through meditation and contemplation so that I can help calm your worries and rekindle your joy."

Pink Tourmaline

Archangels: Chamuel and Jophiel

Healing Properties: As a female balancing stone, this crystal helps you accept devotion and receive universal gifts.

Message: "Call on me when you're searching for love, for I open your heart to free expression and feeling, relieve past wounds, and release that which holds you bound to old patterns. In my presence, you discover a contagious sense of exhilaration."

Watermelon Tourmaline

Archangel: Metatron

Colors: Pink and green

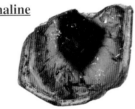

Healing Properties: Watermelon tourmaline blends compassion with passion to create love from the physical and spiritual levels.

Message: "Bringing blessings of love in all manners to those who feel my call, I activate their heart chakra with intensity and speed. My miracle mirrors Divine love through partners, friends, family, and loved ones."

Mineral Name:
Turquoise

Archangel:
Sandalphon

Colors: Blue, green, and turquoise, often with black veins or colorations

Healing Properties: Turquoise blends the energy of Heaven and Earth. This shaman's stone heals the spirit; and induces wisdom, trust, and kindness.

Message: "I'm a shaman's stone throughout the world, bringing the combined blessings of water and sky while reflecting the beauty and bounty of this life. I embody the oneness of Earth and Heaven, and the fountain of healing wisdom beats in my veins. Use me to speak your truth, heal your heart, free your soul, and move forward without fear. Ask for power and guidance, for the ancient ones will heed your call and answer in the rhythm of your being. Sink now into the quiet and allow for your healing."

CRYSTAL CHARTS

ASTROLOGICAL
SUN SIGNS AND
ASSOCIATED STONES

Astrological Sun Sign	Birth Dates	Stone Association
Aries	March 21–April 19	Amethyst, Jasper
Taurus	April 20–May 20	Emerald, Carnelian
Gemini	May 21–June 21	Aquamarine
Cancer	June 22–July 22	Pearl, Moonstone

Leo	July 23–Aug. 22	Ruby, Jade
Virgo	Aug. 23–Sept. 22	Tourmaline, Beryl
Libra	Sept. 23–Oct. 23	Sapphire, Opal
Scorpio	Oct. 24–Nov. 21	Agate, Malachite
Sagittarius	Nov. 22–Dec. 21	Lapis Lazuli, Topaz
Capricorn	Dec. 22–Jan. 19	Turquoise, Garnet
Aquarius	Jan. 20–Feb. 18	Onyx, Clear Quartz
Pisces	Feb. 19–March 20	Coral, Amber

BIRTH MONTH STONES

Birth Month	Stone
January	Garnet
February	Amethyst
March	Aquamarine
April	Diamond
May	Emerald
June	Pearl
July	Ruby
August	Peridot
September	Sapphire
October	Opal
November	Topaz
December	Turquoise

CHAKRA STONES

Chakra Name: Root
Focus: Survival, security, and grounding
Location: Base of the spine
Colors: Red, black
Psychic Focus: Spatial intuition
Stones: Garnet, ruby, red jasper, black tourmaline,
       smoky quartz

Chakra Name: Sacral
Focus: Creativity, sensuality, intimacy, and health
Location: Lower abdomen (below the navel)
Color: Orange
Psychic Focus: Balance
Stones: Amber, citrine, carnelian, orange calcite, topaz

Chakra Name: Solar Plexus
Focus: Confidence, power, and emotional stability
Location: Stomach area
Color: Yellow
Psychic Focus: Healing and teaching power
Stones: Golden topaz, tiger's-eye, citrine

Chakra Name: Heart
Focus: Compassion, unconditional love, and empathy
Location: Center of the chest
Colors: Pink, green
Psychic Focus: Clairsentience and intuition
Stones: Rose quartz, aventurine, kunzite, emerald

Chakra Name: Throat
Focus: Communication, speaking truth, and
spontaneity
Location: Throat
Color: Light blue
Psychic Focus: Expression
Stones: Aquamarine, chrysocolla, lapis lazuli,
sodalite, turquoise

Chakra Name: Third Eye
Focus: Intuition, clarity, and discernment
Location: Center of the forehead
Color: Dark blue, indigo blue
Psychic Focus: Clairvoyance
Stones: Amethyst, blue calcite, lapis lazuli

Chakra Name: Ear
Focus: Hearing and listening
Location: Above each eyebrow

Color: Violet red
Psychic Focus: Clairaudience
Stones: Rutilated quartz, pink tourmaline

Chakra Name: Crown
Focus: Higher Self and spirituality
Location: Top of the head
Colors: White, royal purple
Psychic Focus: Claircognizance
Stones: Amethyst, charoite, clear quartz,
       selenite, sugilite

FENG SHUI CRYSTALS AND STONES

Home harmony is a cornerstone of personal peace—and Feng Shui, the ancient Chinese art of placement, focuses on balance and chi (energy) in the home. Using these serenity principles in conjunction with crystals, you can create a wonderful environment in which to relax and recharge, since placing the stones according to our suggestions will bring additional healing and manifestation energy to those particular parts of your life.

Here are the Feng Shui Bagua Map's life areas:

Life Area	Location	Stone
Helpful People/ Travel	Front Right	Moonstone
Career	Center Front	Black Tourmaline

Skills & Knowledge	Front Left	Lapis Lazuli
Abundance	Left Rear	Amethyst
Fame/ Reputation	Central Rear	Garnet
Relationships/ Love	Right Rear	Rose Quartz
Creativity/ Children	Right Center	Clear Quartz
Family	Left Center	Green Jade
Health/ Harmony	Center	Citrine

A Concise List of Stones and Their Attributes

Agate: Strengthens your mind and body; helps you discern the truth; powerful healing stone when used in conjunction with the chakra-color system.

Agate, Blue Lace: Facilitates calmness; creates a sense of self-awareness that helps maintain balance during times of stress.

Agate, Botswana: Serene movements of blue and gray help soothe your nerves, lift depression, and place your focus on service.

Agate, Crazy Lace: Exceptional tool for reconnecting to Mother Earth; adds a feeling of groundedness when multiple priorities demand your attention.

Agate, Fire: Stone of the astrologer; increases your sense of safety and protection.

Agate, Green Moss: Nature incarnate; creates an immediate bond with the natural world when used as a touchstone; excellent for elementals.

Amber: Ancient manifestation tool; use with focused intention to attain your goals.

Amethyst: Calming, protective jewel; excellent meditation tool; accelerates development of your psychic abilities.

Angelite: Removes fears with calming energy; increases faith and serenity; a perfect choice for astral travel and angelic communication.

Apophyllite: Enhances clairvoyance and assists in out-of-body travel; outstanding meditation stone; links with angelic energy and improves your dream recall.

Aquamarine: Balances your emotional, mental, and physical aspects; creates an awareness and integration of universal truths.

Aventurine: Heals heart pain and accelerates the balancing of your internal yin-and-yang energy.

Azurite: Transformation stone that's linked with creativity, intuition, and inspiration; eliminates illusion.

Azurite and Malachite: Blends the powerful properties of both minerals to create new energy; focuses on accepting your personal power while reducing stress.

Calcite: Symbol of nature incarnate; ideal partner for manifested elementals or those who wish to connect with that realm; creates an immediate bond with the natural world when it's used as a touchstone.

Calcite, Blue: Eases joint pain and unlocks the hidden reason for discomfort.

Calcite, Brown: Acts as a stabilizer when you're faced with conflicting priorities; wonderful for parents and businesspeople.

Calcite, Cream: Assists with astral travel; emotional balancer; creates a sense of lightness and ease.

Calcite, Gray: Establishes focus on being centered in your personal power; produces clear thoughts for decision making.

Calcite, Green: Excellent healer for the physical body; brings Divine flow into your life with ease and harmony.

Calcite, Honey: Helps cleanse toxins and bring your body into alignment for optimal well-being.

Calcite, Orange: Delivers a new awareness and appreciation of creative expression; reminds you to embrace your own abilities.

Calcite, Pink: Clears and rebalances your heart chakra to increase self-love; expands your overall capacity for compassion.

Carnelian: Creates harmony between your mental focus and creative inspiration, allowing your vision to be actualized; wonderful touchstone for artists.

Celestite: Assists with evolution to higher levels of consciousness; serves as a communication tool for linking with angels; heightens awareness of your personal truth.

Charoite: Third-eye stone; enhances psychic awareness and abilities; catalyst for discovering and healing hidden fears.

Chrysanthemum Stone: Stone of change that expands compatibility; builds unity through fun and innocence; removes obstructions and helps you start or continue moving toward your goals.

Chrysocolla: Balances your heart center, which brings stability and awareness of your emotions; focuses the healing energy of universal love into your personal experience.

Chrysocolla and Malachite: Excellent for business; accesses abundance; increases capacity to love; helps break down barriers.

Chrysoprase: A light, joyous crystal that works to heal personal problems; assists in lifting depression with calming, healing energy.

Cinnabar: Often referred to as a merchant stone; promotes profitable business transactions while establishing a sense of abundance.

Citrine: Power alignment tool that works with your Higher Self to heal old patterns; increases self-esteem and attracts abundance.

Copper: Exceptional in easing joint pain; increases self-esteem and self-awareness; establishes emotional boundaries.

Coral: A precious gift from the oceans that supports the healing of bone structures and eases emotional distress.

Danburite: Stone of the shaman; clear, pure, intense energy unlocks barriers and blocks with joy; powerful healing tool best used in conjunction with other crystals.

Desert Rose: Enhances your feelings of well-being; increases your understanding of your unique personal value in the universal plan.

Diamond: Reflects all colors of the rainbow (and chakra system); channels clarity, commitment, and communication; enhances prosperity, love, and spirituality, while also focusing on personal purpose.

Dioptase: Enhances life balance; used to create harmony while working on your personal purpose; powerful healer.

Emerald: Stone of the heart; excellent for dream work and meditation; works to deepen spirituality and consciousness; all-purpose healing gem.

Fluorite: Accesses your deeper awareness and spiritual growth; grounds energy and improves your focus; strong restorative tool.

Garnet: Stimulates passion, creativity, and purpose; assists in healing blood-related disease.

Gold: All-purpose healer; stabilizes, purifies, and balances while presenting the male energy of action to the world; speaks of abundance and well-being.

Hematite: Enhances your personal magnetism, optimism, will, and courage; strengthens your physical and etheric bodies; acts as a grounding tool.

Jade: Prosperity stone that also aids with health; assists with past-life recall and ancient wisdom, especially in Asian traditions.

Jasper: Color family that works with your chakras to balance, recalibrate, and heal; soft energy nurtures and enhances organizational skills and quickens project completion.

Jasper, Ocean: Embodies the heart-healing properties of pink and green; circular markings assist with circular breath and movement of energy.

Jasper, Picture: Perfect companion for bringing nature's therapeutic powers indoors; serves as reminder to embrace meditation practice.

Kunzite: Opens your heart to love; helps create balanced partnerships; promotes peace on Earth by reducing individual separation and stress.

Kyanite: Connects you to youthful zest and optimism; good for speaking from your heart with trust; aids in experiencing the joy of life.

Labradorite: Represents the temple of stars; assists in discovering your destiny; clarifies your inner sight.

Lapis Lazuli: Opens your third eye and expands your senses; connects your heart and head to create balance and interdependence in your relationships.

Larimar: Gentle, innocent energy reminiscent of the unicorn; releases depression with calming energy.

Lemurian Quartz: Rare, powerful crystal that connects you with ancient information from past civilizations; promotes self-confidence through increased focus and concentration; strong telepathic stone and healing partner.

Lepidolite: Relaxing mineral soothes and dissolves stress while supporting the discovery of your Higher Self.

Malachite: Exceptional healer; builds your physical health by strengthening your heart; attracts abundance through your heart's life purpose.

Moldavite: Extraordinary vibration elevates consciousness with awareness; helps you connect with ascended masters.

Moonstone: Stone of new beginnings and talisman of good fortune; encourages positive change; protects travelers.

Obsidian, Black: Nature's shelter for sensitive individuals; dispels negativity and pain; repels unwelcome feelings.

Obsidian, Rainbow: Helpful in understanding the present in terms of the past; helps you release old beliefs and judgments.

Obsidian, Snowflake: Reduces fear and rebalances your focus so that you can concentrate on positive outcomes.

Onyx: Increases your awareness of visions and dreams; emphasizes self-control and grounding; good for individuals who'd like to increase their concentration.

Opal: The essence of harmony; balances all aspects of your body to create a sense of peace.

Pearl: Symbol of integrity, purity, and grace; special conduit to the heavens that works especially well with colored stones.

Peridot: Clears the way for your heart to feel; bolsters prosperity in all areas of life; invaluable for understanding relationships with honesty and integrity.

Platinum: High-level conductor that moves energy at great speeds; particularly effective when combined with diamonds.

Pyrite: Assists in creating earthly abundance; provides stabilizing support during meditation, which increases your ability to balance diverse energies.

Quartz: Draws blessings of all kinds into your life; believed to bring the stars into your soul; enhances your spiritual awareness and intensifies the awakening process; harmonizes energies.

Quartz, Blue: Helpful tool when discussing emotional issues; effective purification agent for cleansing your environment, especially when doing so to support harmonious interactions.

Quartz, Green: Inspires creativity; attracts success and abundance; promotes your intuitive capability coupled with love.

Quartz, Rose: Facilitates heart-healing openings to emotional connection on all levels; focuses energy on self-love; fosters inner peace, tranquility, and healing.

Quartz, Smoky: Superb meditation partner that grounds and centers; helps eliminate fears; enhances your dream awareness.

Quartz, Tangerine: Balances your emotions; calms and soothes while increasing your creativity and receptivity to Divine inspiration.

Rhodocrosite: Eases moments of change; serves as a bridge between upper and lower chakras to create a balanced and loving approach to life.

Rhodonite: Use in toning practices to escalate sounds and amplify connections; effective stone for shedding old patterns and pain.

Ruby: Acts as a strengthener for love; induces awareness of your heart's connections; opens you to self-love in order to receive the devotion of others.

Sapphire: Clears mind chatter; enhances your organizational skills and intuitive abilities.

Selenite: Gives you access to information from the Pleiades; heals negativity and fears; provides alignment and cleansing abilities.

Silver: Feminine, receptive energy that softly engages with stones in order to escalate their properties.

Sodalite: Helps you release control issues; increases psychic awareness; wonderful third-eye stone.

Sugilite: Amplifies pineal and pituitary gland activity to connect your physical and spiritual bodies.

Tiger's-Eye: Enhances connection with your personal power and strengthens your resolve; improves insights and softens stubbornness; fosters self-confidence.

Tiger's-Eye, Red: Builds your confidence by accessing your inner wisdom and guidance; perfect for public speaking.

Topaz: Master stone with a heightened vibration; brings information and healing at an accelerated rate, especially for those with open hearts.

Topaz, Blue: Writers' crystal encourages communication from your heart; aligns your creativity and purpose.

Topaz, Golden: Joyful gem that partners to attract wealth, well-being, and love; helps fully open your crown chakra to heavenly exchange.

Topaz, Pink: Aphrodisiac drawing love on many levels; heart-chakra stone that amplifies your ability to love unconditionally.

Topaz, White: Heightens your vibrational levels; clears old energy and increases your feelings of connection with the Divine.

Tourmaline: Significant clan of healing stones that commands energy on its own; creates a chakra bridge of spiritual expansion when used with other crystals.

Tourmaline, Black: Excels at dispelling negativity in all forms, especially electromagnetic vibrations associated with cell phones and computers; stimulates practicality with creativity so you can achieve your goals.

Tourmaline, Green: Rejuvenating jewel; opens your heart chakra to the joy and zest of life.

Tourmaline, Pink: Female balancer that helps you accept devotion and receive universal gifts.

Tourmaline, Watermelon: Blends compassion and passion to create love from the physical and spiritual levels.

Turquoise: Combines the energies of Heaven and Earth; healer of the spirit that induces wisdom, trust, and kindness; stone of the shaman.

❋
❋ ❋

STONES FOR VARIOUS SITUATIONS, SYMPTOMS, AND DESIRES

Healing Focus	**Stone**
Abundance	Cinnabar, Jade
Abuse	Smoky Quartz
Addictions	Aventurine
Allergies	Chrysocolla
Anorexia	Moss Agate, Rhodocrosite
Anxiety	Citrine, Lapis Lazuli, Smoky Quartz

Appendicitis	Carnelian, Citrine
Appetite, decreasing	Moonstone
Arthritis	Copper, Smoky Quartz
Asthma	Green Tourmaline, Rhodonite
Astral Travel	Angelite, Apophyllite, Green Calcite
Back	Blue Calcite, Golden Topaz
Bladder	Carnelian
Blood	Carnelian, Hematite
Blood Pressure	Dioptase, Turquoise

Bones	Calcite, Gold Tiger's-Eye
Breast	Amethyst, Peridot
Breathing	Amber
Broken Bones	Calcite, Hematite, Dioptase
Broken Heart	Malachite, Pink Topaz, Rose Quartz
Bronchitis	Pyrite, Red Jasper, Rutilated Quartz
Burns	Iris Agate, Sodalite
Business	Cinnabar, Citrine
Calming	Blue Lace Agate, Clear Quartz, Rose Quartz

Cancer	Rhodocrosite, Sugilite
Change	Garnet, Pink Tourmaline, Smoky Quartz
Childbirth	Jasper, Moonstone, Ruby
Child Conception	Coral, Garnet
Circulation	Citrine, Pyrite, Ruby
Clairvoyance	Amethyst, Azurite, Clear Quartz
Colds	Clear or Purple Fluorite
Colic	Jade, Malachite
Colon	Amber, Malachite

Coma	Moldavite
Confidence	Aventurine, Gold
Depression	Azurite, Kunzite, Topaz
Diabetes	Amethyst, Jasper, Malachite
Dog Bite	Amethyst, Carnelian, Dioptase
Dreams	Diamond, Rutilated Quartz
Ears	Amber, Blue Fluorite, Sapphire
Energy, increasing	Amber, Jasper, Peridot
Entity Removal	Obsidian, Onyx
Epilepsy	Moldavite, Jet

Eyes, health of	Aquamarine, Rhodocrosite
Eyesight	Emerald, Fluorite, Rhodocrosite
Feet	Aquamarine, Onyx
Gallbladder	Garnet, Jasper, Malachite
Genitals	Garnet, Obsidian, Smoky Quartz
Grief	Lapis Lazuli, Obsidian, Rose Quartz
Hair	Malachite, Opal, Quartz
Hands	Quartz
Headaches	Amethyst, Blue Lace Agate, Sugilite

Hearing	Lapis Lazuli, Sapphire, Sodalite
Heart	Dioptase, Gold, Peridot
Immune System	Blue Quartz, Lepidolite, Malachite
Impotency	Garnet
Infection	Ruby, Turquoise
Insomnia	Fluorite, Lapis Lazuli, Sodalite
Itching	Azurite, Malachite
Joints	Dioptase, Hematite
Kidneys	Carnelian, Honey Calcite, Jade
Legs	Jade

Life Purpose	Clear Quartz, Emerald
Liver	Azurite and Malachite, Peridot, Rhodocrosite
Lungs	Chrysocolla, Dioptase
Memory	Amber, Fire Agate, Pyrite
Menopause	Garnet, Lapis Lazuli, Moonstone
Menstrual Period	Moonstone, Smoky Quartz
Migraines	Dioptase, Tourmaline
Money Issues	Cinnabar, Citrine, Jade

Mouth	Sodalite
Nails	Calcite, Opal, Pearl
Nightmares	Amethyst, Chalcedony, Rhodonite
Ovaries	Tiger's-Eye, Moonstone
Pain	Malachite, Sugilite
Pancreas	Green Moss Agate
Past Lives	Amethyst, Obsidian
Performance Anxiety	Aquamarine, Moonstone, Red Tiger's-Eye
Pineal Gland	Clear Quartz, Fluorite

Pituitary Gland	Amethyst, Fluorite, Lapis Lazuli
Pregnancy	Dioptase, Rose Quartz
Sinuses	Fluorite
Skin	Azurite and Malachite
Smoking	Amethyst, Aventurine
Spine	Jasper, Labradorite
Stress	Azurite and Malachite, Turquoise
Teeth	Calcite, Fluorite
Throat	Amber, Tourmaline, Turquoise

Thymus	Aquamarine, Rhodocrosite
Thyroid	Chrysocolla, Lapis Lazuli, Peridot
Ulcers	Chrysocolla, Gold Tiger's-Eye, Pyrite
Urinary Tract	Amber, Citrine, Jade
Veins	Aquamarine, Opal
Weight, decreasing	Labradorite
Worry, decreasing	Orange Calcite, Tangerine Quartz

BIBLIOGRAPHY

Bauer, M., *Precious Stones.* New York, NY: Dover Publications, 1968.

Dolfyn, *Crystal Wisdom.* Oakland, CA: Earthspirit Inc., 1989.

Fuller, S., *Rocks & Minerals.* London, UK: Dorling Kindersley Publishing, 1995.

Gardner-Gordon, J., *Color and Crystals: A Journey Through the Chakras.* Freedom, CA: The Crossing Press, 1988.

Hall, J., *The Crystal Bible.* Hampshire, UK: Godsfield Press, 2003.

Kunz, G. F., *The Curious Lore of Precious Stones.*
New York, NY: Dover Publications, 1971.

Kynes, S., *Gemstone Feng Shui.* St. Paul, MN: Llewellyn
Publications, 2002.

Lee, J., *The Crystal and Mineral Guide.* Baldoyle,
Ireland: Aeon Press, 1998.

Raphaell, K., *Crystal Enlightenment.* Santa Fe, NM:
Aurora Press, 1985.

Simpson, L., *The Book of Crystal Healing.* New York,
NY: Sterling Publishing Company, 1997.

Thompson, H. L., *Legends of Gems.* Los Angeles, CA:
Graphic Press, 1937.

Blessings and Gratitude to the Following Individuals...

. . . from Doreen Virtue:

Thank you to Louise L. Hay; Reid Tracy; Jill Kramer; Christy Salinas; Amy Rose Grigoriou; Lisa Iris; Steven Farmer; Shankari; Hermes/Thoth; the angelic, ascended-master, and elemental kingdoms; EarthWorks; and to the Light and Love within everyone and everything.

. . . from Judith Lukomski:

I am eternally thankful for the loving guidance of God, the angels, ascended masters, and the mineral kingdom. With joy, I acknowledge those who've played a role in this project. Each provided a unique gift at the perfect moment:

Doreen, you embody love, inspiring through your work and actions. Collaborating with you to share the message of crystal power has proven to be exciting and a lot of fun! Thanks to the Hay House team for their dedication to excellence and commitment to producing tools of empowerment. Cheryl Maneff, your photographic artistry captured the unique beauty and personality of each stone. Ken Lauher of Ken's Jeweler's of Laguna Beach, the rare selections from your personal collection are a stunning display of nature's art.

A special thanks to the crystals, teachers, and guardians I've met along the way. I appreciate your generosity in sharing wisdom with enthusiasm. Lots of love to my family: Benjamin, Irene, Jeffery, Steve; and a special thanks to my sister Barbara for her perspective. I'm blessed to share the adventure with dear friends who surround me with love, laughter, and light: Chris and Mark Marmes, Lynnette Brown, Angie Hartfield, Laura Underwood, Scott Bishop, James and Debra Fitts, Gayle Greco, Nigel and Ann Griffiths, plus my Colorado connections—I thank you.

To the Angel Therapy Practitioner community, the Chakra Shack, and all the wonderful individuals whom I've met doing angel readings and intuitive consultations, I'm honored to know you. Finally, to you readers, it's a privilege to be part of your crystal connection—remember: have fun! I'm wishing everyone the blessings of Heaven and Earth today. Namaste.

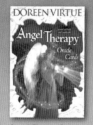

ABOUT THE AUTHORS

Doreen Virtue, Ph.D., is a doctor of psychology who works with the angelic realm. She uses crystals in her personal and professional work, which she discussed in her book *Angel Medicine.* Doreen is the author of numerous best-selling books and products, including the *Healing with the Angels* book and oracle cards.

She has appeared on *Oprah,* CNN, *Good Morning America,* and in newspapers and magazines worldwide. Doreen also teaches classes related to her books. For information on her products, workshops, message-board community, or to receive her free monthly e-newsletter, please visit **www.angeltherapy.com**.

Judith Lukomski is a gifted intuitive, crystal energy healer, teacher, and speaker. With a lifelong commitment to spiritual development, along with a successful background in business management and psychology, she provides practical tools for integrating metaphysical principles into everyday life. Judith shares a unique connection with crystal energy. She partners with the angelic, elemental, and ascended masters realms, acting as a channel to deliver insights supporting personal growth and empowerment.

For information regarding individual consultations, personal stone selections, crystal and intuitive development workshops, certification programs, and publications, please visit **www.crystalfriends.com**. Share your crystal stories with Judith at: **mystory@crystalfriends.com** or contact her via mail at: P.O. Box 4017, Dana Point, CA 92629 USA.

∏OTES

NOTES

NOTES

NOTES

NOTES

NOTES

HAY HOUSE TITLES
OF RELATED INTEREST

Aura-Soma,
by Irene Dalichow and Mike Booth

Aromatherapy A–Z,
by Connie and Alan Higley, and Pat Leatham

Feng Shui Dos & Taboos for Health & Well-Being,
by Angi Ma Wong

Getting in the Gap (book-with-CD),
by Dr. Wayne W. Dyer

Heal Your Body,
by Louise L. Hay

Sylvia Browne's Book of Angels,
by Sylvia Browne

The Western Guide to Feng Shui—Room by Room,
by Terah Kathryn Collins

❀

All of the above are available at your local bookstore,
or may be ordered by contacting Hay House.

We hope you enjoyed this Hay House book. If you'd like to receive our online catalog featuring additional information on Hay House books and products, or if you'd like to find out more about the Hay Foundation, please contact:

HAY HOUSE

Hay House, Inc.
P.O. Box 5100
Carlsbad, CA 92018-5100

(760) 431-7695 or **(800) 654-5126**
(760) 431-6948 (fax) or **(800) 650-5115 (fax)**
www.hayhouse.com® • **www.hayfoundation.org**

※

Published and distributed in Australia by:
Hay House Australia Pty. Ltd. • 18/36 Ralph St. • Alexandria NSW
2015 *Phone:* 612-9669-4299 • *Fax:* 612-9669-4144 •
www.hayhouse.com.au

Published and distributed in the United Kingdom by:
Hay House UK, Ltd. • 292B Kensal Rd., London W10 5BE
Phone: 44-20-8962-1230 • *Fax:* 44-20-8962-1239 • www.hayhouse.co.uk

Published and distributed in the Republic of South Africa by:
Hay House SA (Pty), Ltd., P.O. Box 990, Witkoppen 2068
Phone/Fax: 27-11-467-8904 • info@hayhouse.co.za
www.hayhouse.co.za

Published in India by:
Hay House Publishers India, Muskaan Complex, Plot No. 3, B-2,
Vasant Kunj, New Delhi 110 070 • *Phone:* 91-11-4176-1620
Fax: 91-11-4176-1630 • www.hayhouse.co.in

Distributed in Canada by:
Raincoast • 9050 Shaughnessy St., Vancouver, B.C. V6P 6E5
Phone: (604) 323-7100 • *Fax:* (604) 323-2600 • www.raincoast.com

※

Take Your Soul on a Vacation

Visit **www.HealYourLife.com**® to regroup, recharge, and reconnect with your own magnificence. Featuring blogs, mind-body-spirit news, and life-changing wisdom from Louise Hay and friends.

Visit **www.HealYourLife.com** today!